RESEARCH DONE RIGHT

How to Get Your Chemical or Plastic to Market Faster

By
Teresa M. O'Brien

To the previous researchers
Whose shoulders we stand on today
and
To the readers who will do
Great things because they took action

Disclaimer and Terms of Use Agreement

RESEARCH DONE RIGHT

TABLE OF CONTENTS

Introduction

This book is designed for you -- the scientist or engineer who is new to commercial research in the chemicals and plastics industry and wants to be effective in commercializing a successful research project.

The process for developing any product is dependent upon the type of product being developed. Developing a chemical will be different from developing an airplane, for example. Therefore, this book is focused on developing chemical and plastics products, since this is where my experience lies.

This book will provide a perspective of how a successful project comes together, thus increasing the odds of your project being successful. It will also give you a "big picture" look at technical research in the commercial world and link that picture to what you do every day.

Academic scientists think in terms of making wonderful scientific discoveries. But in the business world, science isn't just about making scientific discoveries, it's about making money. When scientists fail to understand the unique challenges of working in a corporate environment, they can quickly find themselves engaged in unproductive and unsuccessful projects.

Most of the experiments that scientists might have conducted in an academic environment were under controlled conditions and pre-tested for delivering the desired results. Usually no customer was involved to explain how the end product must perform, there was no requirement to make the product in large volumes, nor was there any requirement to make it cheaper once in production.

However, these commercial challenges are real ones that scientists face when doing product development research for a company. They want to develop a new product or technology that will have great commercial applicability for their company. It takes more than just understanding and applying science to make that happen.

It requires an understanding of the implications of a company's need to make a profit. Yet most scientists have little or no training or understanding of the business side of things, and they typically don't understand the full implications of how the profit motive influences a company's research programs.

Profit is the money remaining after total costs are deducted from total revenue. Profitability margin is a ratio of profit divided by sales. It measures how much of every dollar of sales a company actually keeps in earnings.

Your company is spending significant amounts of money on research and development activities. The expectation is that the results of your scientific efforts will yield profitable sales of product. Profitability will occur when the ideas that you develop:
- meet marketplace needs;
- are offered at a price the market is willing and able to pay; and
- are below your company's total cost to produce.

With someone to help guide you through the landmines, product development becomes much easier and more fun. It is my hope that by reading this book, you will be able to more quickly and successfully develop as a technical researcher in the business world.

One way to think of your task as a researcher is that you are creating a "greased chute" so that once your product is developed, it moves forward through the commercialization process as smoothly and quickly as possible.

This book is about helping you, the researcher, move your project forward faster – resulting in lower cost and higher value. This book also gives you some specific areas to consider for reading, learning, and planning that are likely to bear fruit.

Although you may not be personally responsible (especially in large companies) for acquiring all of the non-scientific information outlined in this book, it is your responsibility to know and understand it well enough to make informed decisions on your experiments.

Time is precious to a company, and reducing the amount of time to acquire the research knowledge needed to develop a successful project is gold to your company.

Fundamentally, your company exchanges time and money for useful knowledge, so that your company can ultimately make a profit from commercialized product or service. Some of that knowledge was acquired when they hired you, some from previous research, and some from new experiments.

Staying focused on minimizing the development timeline is key. You and your team are likely to make not only a better product but get it done faster by asking questions, thinking things through, and planning.

This time focus can be summarized by understand the critical path and then do everything you can to minimize the time your activities are on the critical path. (The critical path is the sequence of <u>activities</u> in a <u>project plan</u> which must be <u>completed</u>. It identifies the minimum amount of time needed for completion of the project.)

The world is constantly changing. New customer needs continually arise. For example, a company may want to develop a new product, and this can sometimes require a change in material to meet that need. Since the business world is moving at an ever-faster pace, the response by suppliers to customer needs also has to get faster. In a world of instant tweets, text messages, pictures, and videos, we have all become used to a fast response. Your ability to be adaptive and efficient will be a key to your success in the corporate environment.

When companies make product line changes, they usually establish timelines to make those changes. Sometimes those timelines are externally imposed by their customers. Having a product offering available that will meet your customer's performance requirements in a timeframe that meets their evaluation and production schedule can be of great value.

If you miss either your customer's evaluation or production window, your company won't get the business – not this year, and maybe not *ever*. Once your customer has found a new product and it is working well, your customer will spend their time and resources on other issues that need their attention.

There are three major categories of product development in the chemical and plastics industry. One category is a minor modification of an existing product (perhaps to get a little easier flow during processing). The second one is a major revamp of an existing product. The third category is the development of a product that is new to the company and new to the world.

Because this book describes the general process for developing a product, it will have applicability to all three categories. It is possible the book may be most useful for the second and third categories where the development time will be longer. Both of these categories require more interactions and communications with others.

How the book is laid out: The beginning chapters of the book discuss the process of developing and commercializing new chemical and plastics products, the typical organizational structures that companies use to support the day-to-day development activities, and the typical decision making structure for moving projects forward. The following chapters address factors external to the company and factors internal to the company. The remaining chapters address additional product development issues, plus information specific to new-to-the-world products and to products undergoing major modifications.

At the end of each chapter, I have listed questions that are designed to help you get a clearer picture of your development project. Many of the answers to these questions can be obtained in discussions with your team members. Some may require external input. I encourage you to seek the answers internally first from the appropriate team members.

The macro process for understanding product development and commercialization (as described in Chapter 1, How a Successful Product Comes Together) is the same for any industry. Regardless of the industry:

- they all have competition;
- there is a relentless aging of products (each having its own unique product life cycle);
- manufacturers continuously look for ways to reduce manufacturing costs;
- there is constant renewal of products ;
- products must be fairly priced before customers will purchase ;
- there are innovators, early adopters, early majority, late majority, and laggards of customer adoption of new products;
- a competitive advantage is important when competing for market share; and
- speed to market is becoming more important.

Therefore, your development team will need to assess whether you can develop your product faster, better, and cheaper to obtain an acceptable share of the market. For the chemical industry, some of the major focuses of product development tend to be on intellectual property, environmental, health, and safety issues.

What are my qualifications to write in this field? I have lived it and done it. I completed a ten year research project in only three years. I have been on both the commercial and technical side of product development. I have been a member of, a leader of, and coached teams doing product development.

But most importantly, I had a mindset of accelerating product development. I found ways to get my projects developed faster. I believed that the company hired me as a researcher to help it make a profit.

Because I had this mindset of helping the company make money, I was always looking for ways to become more efficient in my work. As a result, I sought out collaboration with experts or experienced people regarding specific components of the project. When I was told to build a small lab

x

reactor, for example, I constructed one based on my collaborations with other experts, observed their reactors, and then determined the required components to be used.

In that case, I leveraged knowledge. My approach today continues to be about leveraging existing knowledge and experience – wherever it's found – to move ahead as quickly and easily as possible, with a minimum of backtracking.

Keeping in mind the principle that "time is money," I emphasized a number of objectives in my projects:
- Being clear on the definition of success for the project
- Looking for any leveragable pieces of information or opportunity for my project
- Leveraging that information
- Time sequencing activities to go faster
- Anticipating problems and developing contingencies to minimize problems
- Communicating
- Teamwork
- Product development timeline planning
- Obtaining management support from the beginning of the project

This book is a condensation of my learning and approach as a researcher, product development team lead, and team coach. It contains ideas and suggestions that will increase the speed of both the completion of your projects and their odds for success. I wish you the best of thought, hard work, and luck. For in research, you often need all three!

Part 1

How a Successful Project Comes Together

1 -- Development Process

A project is financially successful if your company can make a profit from your product, after factoring in all the development and production costs. This usually requires that a new product has to be of greater benefit to the customer than what is currently available – either lower purchase price or better performance or both.

Therefore, your product has to create value in the marketplace. Whenever a solution is found that will fulfill an unmet market need, an opportunity for creating value has been found (see Figure 1.1). Scientific success is a prerequisite for commercial success.

FIGURE 1.1 How Value Is Created

The development process usually starts in one of two ways: (1) a customer articulates a need to a supplier who may or may not have a product on hand to address the need; or (2) a supplier develops a new product or technology and searches for a market need for the product. After an opportunity has been identified, a number of scientific activities have to be completed before a product is commercialized, as shown in Figure 1.2 below.

FIGURE 1.2 How a Development Project Comes Together (Process Steps)

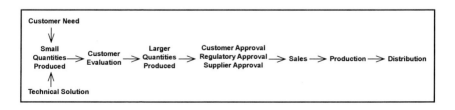

First, small laboratory quantities of the product are usually made for preliminary testing and evaluation by selected customers, usually under secrecy and non-analysis agreements.

In what may well turn out to be an iterative process, the customer gives the supplier feedback for further improvement of the product. Once preliminary testing identifies a potential solution, larger quantities of the material are made for further customer evaluation and approval, along with any regulatory approval that's needed.

Simultaneously, the supplier's production plant and supply chain management will verify the scalability of the product to large scale production, determine the economics of production, approve any raw material suppliers, and address shipping and packaging procedures. This information, plus the selling price and sales volume of the product, will allow the supplier to assess whether this will be an economically viable opportunity for the company.

Once the supplier, customer, and regulatory groups approve the product and a sales contract has been negotiated, the production plant can begin shipping the product.

As you can see from just this high level overview of the product development process, there are many entities that will have requirements and concerns about any product that is going to be commercialized. Competitors' responses, company research funding, product pricing, and marketplace windows of opportunity – to name just a few variables – will need to be addressed by your Product Development Team as you work to bring a product to market.

Before we address each of these factors, we will look at various support structures that an organization typically has for doing product development: the multi-functional teams that companies use to develop products, the product development work process (including project planning) that companies have documented using the expertise of experienced product developers in their organizations, and the decision process (including stage gates) that companies use to move projects forward in the development process. This, plus the previous overview of how products are developed, will provide the basic framework from which we can focus on doing product development faster.

2 -- Multi-Functional Product Development Teams

When business management in medium to large companies decides to fund a development project, the first thing they do is assign individuals from various functions within the business to be members of the Product Development Team. Typically, the core of the team will contain a representative from each of these functions: research, technical customer interface, marketing, production, and finance. Usually, but not always, the marketing representative leads the team.

Initially, the team will be fairly small, and most of the team members will not be assigned full time to the project. As the project moves forward, more team members will be added, and more members will have the project as a full-time responsibility.

FIGURE 2.1 Team Interactions

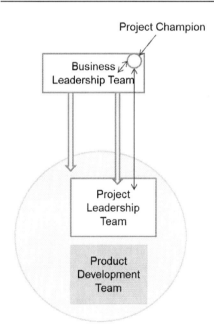

Typically, a member of Business Management will be assigned the role of Project Champion for the project. The Champion is the eyes and ears of Business Management for the assigned project and represents the progress and issues of the Product Development Team to the authorizing Business Management. The Project Champion is the focal point of communication for a given project between Business Management and the Project Leadership Team. See Figure 2.1.

Once the project has more than a few members, Business Management will identify members of the Product Development Team who will become the Project Leadership Team for the project. The Project Leadership Team members usually already have a significant amount of their time assigned to the project, so this assignment is a logical extension of the work they are already doing.

The Project Leadership Team is responsible for coordinating activities and communicating results and changes in direction to the rest of the Product Development Team members. The Project Leadership Team also communicates with the Project Champion. This results in transparency of progress and allows the project to move forward as efficiently and effectively as possible.

The Project Leadership Team will coordinate the project activities so that no one part gets too far in front of the rest and so information flows freely among the members of the group. The project plan that the Product Development Team puts together for the project greatly aids the Product Development Team.

In the early stages, the Product Development Team refines the scope of the project and the potential opportunity, so that Business Leadership can determine whether this project idea is something that really fits the strategic direction of the business. If the project does, then the Project Leadership Team coordinates activities to assess whether the project will be economically viable. This includes defining a project plan for addressing the opportunity, identifying critical hurdles that may impede success, and estimating profitability. If management agrees that a product is worth developing after this preliminary assessment, then multi-functional coordination really ratchets up.

As the project moves from shaping and defining an opportunity to executing the development program, some of the Product Development Team may change to reflect the revision in needed skills.

When a project moves into full-scale development, the emphasis shifts from the research group developing and designing a product to the commercial group getting customer trials and approvals of the product. Simultaneously manufacturing will be finalizing a production process and the finance department will be refining the economics. The role of finance is especially critical if the project will require going to the capital board for a capital authorization (usually for funds to build or modify a production plant).

As the project moves closer to commercialization, the number of people involved in the project increases. This means that the Project Leadership Team will be spending more of their time, perhaps as much as 100%, on this project as they shepherd it through commercial launch.

Once the project is launched and customers are buying the product consistently, the Project Leadership Team will start to transition the product from a development project to day-to-day operations. These handoffs are typically well orchestrated and happen over months. Each function will have its own transfer plan, based on the project's need for special handling during the transition. These transfer plans include transitioning Product Development Team members to other opportunities in the company. The Project Leadership Team oversees the transition to make sure it happens in a timeframe that is right for the project's success.   Once the transition has occurred, the Product Development Team, including the Project Leadership Team, will disband.

In larger, established companies, the Project Leadership Team is responsible for making sure the project is well documented, including developing a lessons learned assessment of the project for use by future development teams. The Project Leadership Team is also responsible for making sure that there is reward and recognition of individual and team efforts throughout the project, including a celebration of the project success at the end of commercialization.

Because product development has many unknowns that need to be addressed, there will often be hurdles that develop which the Project Leadership Team will need to jointly discuss and determine how to resolve. All of this activity requires that the Project Leadership Team be able to work well together, seek advice, and communicate any changes to others in their functions. Each Project Leadership Team member also needs to be effective enough on the Leadership Team to be able to represent the interests of their function at the Project Leadership Team meetings.

In newer, smaller companies that may be working on their first product(s), the whole company may be part of the development team and each team member may wear multiple hats. The development process may also be less formalized. Regardless of the formality of the work process and the size of the Project Development Team, all the development work needs to be completed for a product to be commercialized.

Usually in a small company, all the team members will know each other and work in close proximity to each other. If the company is new enough, it might not have full-time employees to handle all the roles (e.g. patent attorney), so there may be members from outside the company with whom the team will work.

QUESTIONS TO ASK:
- Who is the Project Champion for your project?
- Who are the members of the Project Leadership Team?
- Who else is on the Product Development Team?

3 -- How Project Planning Works

Since time is money, wasting time wastes money. Therefore, it is important to work in a manner that minimizes elapsed time (the time from when a task is started to when it is completed) to maximize success. You need to develop a bias for reducing elapsed time, not just work activity. Focusing on elapsed time is important as customers demand faster response times between their initial request for a solution and the delivery of the solution.

Because reducing time to market can be gold to a company, Gantt charts from project planning tools (such as Microsoft Project) are often used. These tools are useful in determining a task-by-task Project Plan and the least amount of time and money it will take to complete a project. This shortest time is called the *critical path*. Because these combined tasks determine the <u>length</u> of the project, increasing the amount of time it takes to complete any tasks that are on the critical path will automatically increase the project completion time. Note: the tasks on the critical path say nothing about the difficulty or importance of each task to the overall project. Your company will likely have a project planning tool they prefer to use.

The Project Plan provides details of what needs to be done, by whom, and when. The Project Leadership Team will coordinate the development of a Project Plan for your project. This usually develops over a series of discussions and meetings so that all team members, not just the leadership team, have input into developing the plan.

Once all the known tasks are depicted in the initial project plan, the team works to minimize the time needed to complete the project in order to meet the required timeframe (Rarely will the initial sequence of activities meet the target deadline). Discussion will primarily center around activities that are on the critical path.

Reducing the time to complete a task on the critical path will shorten the overall time to complete the project UNTIL another task or tasks become the rate determining task(s). At that point, your project will then have a new critical path. The Product Development Team will continue to modify the plan to achieve an acceptable project completion date. This is an iterative process throughout the project as more information becomes known about the timing of specific work.

An example can help illustrate how a project critical path can be shortened. Let's start with the work being done in series (Figure 3.1).

FIGURE 3.1 Project Steps Completed in Series

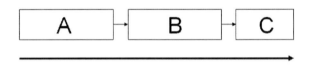

Let's assume that all the work has to be done, and it will take the indicated amount of elapsed time to do the work. (The length of each block represents time to complete each activity.) The solid line at the bottom is our marker for the amount of total <u>elapsed</u> time that is required for all the work.

If a way can be found to do even one of the activities in parallel with another, the elapsed time (and, therefore, the critical path) will shorten for the total work to be completed, even if the total AMOUNT of work that needs to be done is not reduced. This is represented below.

FIGURE 3.2 Doing Two Steps in Parallel

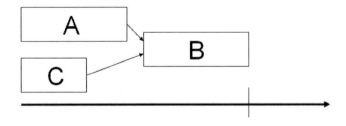

In this case, we have activities A and C being done in parallel. This rearrangement of activity is one that many researchers are familiar with. But there are still other options to consider.

If part of one activity can be unbundled from the rest of the activity, the project time line can potentially be reduced. This type of situation is useful when one person or function needs only <u>part</u> of the output of another's work to get started on their longer lead time work. By understanding what output the person needs first and figuring out how to get that information completed earlier, sometimes the whole process can be moved forward faster. This is shown in Figure 3.2.

FIGURE 3.3 Breaking Activities Apart

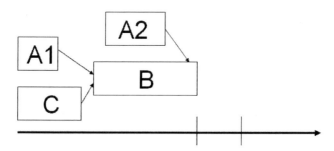

Once again, the same amount of work to complete the project is being done, but because activity A is now divided into two parts, we are able to cut the total <u>elapsed</u> time for the project (and the critical path is shortened).

Understanding how to effectively split a task can require input from multiple members of the team. The best way to get this input is to ask those who will be using your output what information they need to begin their work.

For example, long lead time items, such as reactors, are often ordered without knowing the final exact product recipe. There are only a limited number of material choices that engineers will realistically have to choose from, and the process parameters for the various construction materials have relatively large gaps in performance. Therefore, engineering can quickly focus in on the choice of one or two materials of construction and develop any experiments needed to finalize the reactor choice. Thus, engineering can place the order for the reactor earlier and save time on building or modifying a plant.

There is yet another way to reduce how long it takes for a project to be completed. This is to find another way to get to the end result, rather than doing steps A, B, and C.

This is represented in the next drawing (Figure 3.4). An example of this might be licensing a piece of non-critical technology, rather than developing your own in-house.

FIGURE 3.4 An Alternate Path

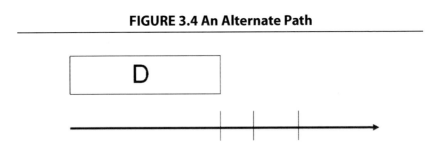

By making adjustments to our project steps, the amount of elapsed time it would take to complete our simple example project is reduced by 50%.

Your project may not have that much time reduction, but it is often worth spending a few hours with the key players looking at the current plan and thinking through how to reduce the total elapsed time to complete the project. Some surprising solutions can unfold, including a different route from the originally proposed solution.

Your company's product development process can be useful in creating the Project Plan. Make sure you review and use your company's development process, including all the flow charts, algorithms, resource utilization guidelines, and any other tools that come along with it.

If nothing else, you will learn more about the handoffs between people and departments and what information is needed. This discussion with all of your internal "customers" (those who will be receiving the output of your work) can be very rewarding in terms of how you do your research and how you communicate it. In the process, you will have established a stronger working relationship with your colleagues because you have asked about their concerns and needs.

Teams that use critical path planning (mostly used with new-to-the-world and larger modified products) spend time thinking through how to shorten the time spent on the critical path, in a fashion similar to what we discussed above. One question everyone should ask: when any of my tasks appears on the critical path, what can I do to either get it off the critical path or reduce the amount of time my task is on the critical path? If each person on the team does this, the project will be completed in the shortest amount of time.

The project planning software can really help keep the project on track. First, you will know what the critical path is and how long it will take you to complete the project. Then you can work to minimize the time to complete the project.

Second, the critical path can determine whether your project is making progress or if this is just an illusion of progress. By pushing hard to do parts of the project that aren't on the critical path while ignoring parts that are (or are about to become) on the critical path, work on your project is not being done as efficiently as possible.

Therefore, getting as much input about product performance as you can, as early as you can, from internal (other departments in your company) and external (customers, regulatory bodies, shareholders) sources can pay big dividends. You won't have as many of the "re-do" loops, which always extend the time of the project.

If the target product performance profile changes late in the development process, this will typically put the completion of the research back on the critical path as other groups wait for that output to complete (or re-do) their work.

QUESTIONS TO ASK:
- What is the timeline and Project Plan for your project?
- What is the critical path for your project?
- What can you do differently to shorten your work that's on the critical path?
- Is there any part of your work that can be taken off the critical path?
- How often should you review the critical path?
- Is the team focused on completing the tasks that are on the critical path?

4 -- Decision Teams and Stage Gates

Companies are reluctant to initially make a large financial commitment on a new product but are willing to make a series of increasingly larger financial investments, as long as the project shows continued commercial viability.

Therefore, many companies use a series of financial decisions to support the funding of a development project. In many cases, a stage gate decision process is employed. Each of the major segments of the project between the funding decisions is called a stage. The funding decision points are referred to as stage gates because the door to further funding for the project can swing open or closed.

The concept is to have interim checkpoints throughout the development process that allow management to decide whether to continue funding a project, to agree upon achievements (sometimes called milestones) necessary for further funding, and then to let the Product Development Team move forward, as long as they are delivering against the agreements.

This allows Business Management to screen out projects early that will not be successful so that resources can be focused on those projects having the best chance for success. Each stage (usually there are four to six stages) will require progressively greater performance information with higher levels of certainty around the answers.

An example of one generic stage gate decision process is shown below.

FIGURE 4.1 Example Stage Gate Decision Process Map

| Verify Strategic Fit | → | Identify Critical Issues | → | Resolve Critical Issues, Develop Prototype | → | Develop Commercially Viable Product | → | Commercialize Product |

By working this way, a company can generate many ideas that will initially be screened (using relatively few resources) to determine the more viable projects. Only then will the company begin to spend the larger development dollars. If progress on the project milestones begins to seriously lag, management will decide whether funding should be terminated for the project.

The stage gate decision criteria are usually spelled out by each business, including any company-specific requirements. Because multiple functions were represented during the development of your company's stage gate process, the decision criteria at each stage will reflect their concerns. Most businesses have three elements to the stage gate decision criteria: (1) the actual criteria (e.g. > 1 million pound opportunity); (2) the weighting factor (e.g.10% for all ten criteria); and (3) level of confidence around values (e.g. 20% probability). Therefore, as a researcher new to product development, be sure to understand the decision criteria needed for each stage gate decision, including the levels of detail and the degree of certainty. This information can be obtained from your Project Leader, your senior R&D member on the development team, or your supervisor. This will keep you from doing too much in one area and missing other criteria altogether. (It takes a lot of resources just to get to 30 – 50% confidence level for a new product.)

Early stage criteria are usually focused on assessing whether the project is a strategic fit for your company, based on your company's strategy and the target markets. An analysis of strengths, weaknesses, opportunities, threats, and trends (SWOTT) relative to this opportunity is helpful in assessing the strategic fit. The first stage will rarely require many experiments to reach a decision point.

Effort is also directed at understanding how the company could make money with the project. This might include the analysis of competitive offerings, a proposed market strategy, a hypothesized technical solution, a hypothesized competitive advantage, an estimate of the cost to develop the product and markets, and an assessment of net present value of the project or other economic metric based on the above information.

If the potential viability of the project is considered acceptable, the focus shifts to creating a prototype product to get marketplace verification of performance and economics. It is in the prototype/sample development stage that the level of funding by the company will increase significantly. Now, among other activities, your company will be running experiments, the patent department will be addressing intellectual property protection, your sales organization will have more meetings with the targeted customers, and, possibly, larger sample quantities of material will be needed.

Every research project has some areas that will prove to be more difficult to develop. When these areas represent a large enough hurdle, they can be considered potential "show stoppers." Some companies call them "critical issues" or "critical success factors." Regardless of what they are called, if a way to resolve those issues is not determined, the project will not be commercialized. It is usually in the prototype development phase that potential "show stoppers" for the project are verified and resolved.

Part of your responsibility is to *identify* potential technical "show stoppers." Articulate the issues as clearly as possible to your Product Development Team early in the research work, and then develop a plan of action that will resolve them. This will give you the maximum amount of time to think about and develop solutions.

Don't be afraid that identifying and articulating the potential show stoppers will immediately kill your project. Most projects have a few potential show stoppers based on a well thought out project plan to which all involved members have contributed.

If your team does not address the show stoppers until the end of the project, and they aren't resolved, your team could waste a lot of company money that might be better spent elsewhere.

Stating the issues early and putting together a plan to address them gives management time to adjust to the potential issues and be reassured as progress is made on addressing them. Contrast this to a huge unknown that "suddenly" crops up late in the project. Management will then start to wonder if it will be solved in time. What else haven't they been told? Should they pull the plug on the project?

Conflicting requirements can sometimes be potential project show stoppers. For example, the customer may require 100 pounds of your material in the next three months, but you can't make that amount fast enough in the lab, and you don't have a pilot plant in your company to make larger amounts of the material. Looking for creative ways to resolve these situations is an important part of developing the new product. (In our example, we could consider outsourcing the manufacture of the 100 pounds to a contract manufacturer.)

Talking with others and reading available literature will help you figure out a starting point for addressing the issue. You might also develop alternate (contingency) plans, in case the first approach proves to be unsuccessful. Since "Plan A" frequently doesn't work, it's worth the mental exercise to develop a contingency plan.

The last stage is the commercial rollout of your product to the marketplace. In this stage, product sales increase and the number of production runs increase. This is where any production lot-to-lot reproducibility issues will be defined and addressed. Each function will also execute their plans of transitioning their responsibilities from a development project focus (with extra testing and monitoring) to day-to-day operations and control.

Some researchers get emotionally attached to their projects and feel that they themselves have failed if their project doesn't make it through every stage gate. It's easy to reach that point, especially if you have worked passionately on the project.

But remember that you are there to help the company make money. If after all your hard work, the project only looks marginally like it *might* be good, but not great, the odds are it won't be successful. Usually the value of the opportunity to the company shrinks the further you progress down the development path and additional market realities are factored in.

Look at the presentations of other researchers on other product development projects to further understand what is expected at each stage gate. Find one or two to model. Talk to the researchers who created these presentations for their insights.

Present your data in a way that makes it easy for the decision makers to assess whether your project meets their criteria. Don't make it difficult for them to figure out. Confusion and uncertainty increase the odds that they will say no. Make it easier for them to say yes.

Some groups use a rigorous decision process with a detailed spreadsheet. Others just vote yes (to continue) or no (to abandon the effort), without completing a formal weighted analysis.

QUESTIONS TO ASK:
- Does your company use a stage gate decision process? What are the decision criteria for your project?
- What are the potential technical show stoppers with your project?
- What is your plan to address these issues?

5 -- Product Development Work Process

Most companies have an established product development work process. The purpose of this documented work process is to provide a standardized approach for all development projects to ensure that they meet all specified requirements. By understanding this rigorous and complete process, future projects' success will be greatly enhanced.

These work processes provide a roadmap for thinking through your current development project. They are a best practice look at the way to do effective and efficient product development in your organization. They show handoffs of work from one function in the organization to another, which is a wonderful resource for you to determine who needs to be notified of your output/results.

These documents contain the knowledge and experience of the most experienced product developers in your organization. They also often contain forms (templates) and established guidelines that new product developers will find helpful.

Therefore, reviewing and understanding your company's Product Development Work Process is an opportunity to learn from your company's master product developers. This Work Process can be used as a checklist to make sure you aren't missing some company-and department-specific requirements.

Some Project Development Work Processes are structured well enough, and integrated effectively with other key company processes that they can be used as a starting template to prepare a detailed task-by-task Project Plan for a development project. Many of the outside agencies (FDA and EPA, for example.) that you will need to work with will be identified in the work process. If your company does not have a formal plan, you can use this book as a starting point for a development process.

Many companies have incorporated Six Sigma and other process optimization tools. These tools are designed to help reduce waste in the process and are best practices that your company and others have found useful.

Six Sigma is more than a set of tools, it is also a mindset. If your company uses Six Sigma in its work processes, you will receive detailed training on the Six Sigma methodology. For the purposes of this book, just know that the tools and techniques that your organization has adopted as a result of process optimization methods will be beneficial to you as you move through the development process.

QUESTIONS TO ASK:
- What is your company's Product Development Work Process?
- What information in the Product Development Work Process can you use in your research?

Part 2

What External Requirements Does Your Product Need to Meet?

6 -- How to Determine What's Driving Your Customers' Need for Your Product

It is important that your team works on applications that will have growth potential for many years. Your company wants to enjoy long term sales so it can recover its development costs and make an acceptable profit.

Therefore, it's best to work on projects that are a strategic fit with where both your company and your target customers are heading. Strategic projects are especially likely to get management's time and attention. They will receive resources as needed and will likely be supported during an economic downturn.

Before your company will commit to funding a new product, detailed market research will be conducted. There must be a high need for the product, and it must be a high priority with your target customers. Your company will not want to commit large amounts of its limited resources to a project that your customers aren't strongly interested in.

Your sales and marketing representatives will be responsible for determining whether this potential product has high importance to your customer. Both your company and your customer will devote sufficient resources to complete the project in a timely manner. The higher the importance the project has to your target customers, the less vulnerable the project will be to funding cuts by them.

If customers have no strong need for this product, there will be no support for trialing the new product at *their* customers. You and your company will have wasted development time and resources on a project that goes nowhere. Plus there is the opportunity cost – your company could have been using those resources on a project with confirmed interest and multi-level support by the customer.

Understanding the primary driver of your customer's need for your new product will give your team a better idea of how strong the need is. It will also keep your team watching for changes that may alter the strength of the need for your product. For example, if your customer is looking for a product to meet a pending change of legislation, the urgency will go away if the implementation of that legislation is significantly delayed or abandoned.

Usually, when a customer has expressed a need for a product, it is because one or more of these situations has occurred:

- *Their* customer is asking for the improvement.
- Your customer, or their customer, is being squeezed on profit margins.
- Your customer, or their customer, is trying to maintain share against new technology.
- Your customer wants an alternate source of supply to a competitor's product for leverage in price negotiations and to minimize production downtime risk if the other supplier has an outage.
- Your customer is anticipating a change in marketplace requirements, usually because of a change in legislation or technology.
- Your customer believes this product will help move them into the #1 or #2 position in the market segment.
- Your customer is #1 in the marketplace and is trying to maintain share with a new and improved product.

As a researcher, you will be developing products to provide solutions to unmet market needs indentified by your sales and marketing organization. The requirements will generally fall into one of the following categories (see Figure 6.1):

- A. Incumbent product pricing with incumbent product performance (alternate source of supply)
- B. Lower priced product with incumbent product performance
- C. Lower priced product with lower performance than incumbent product (down engineering)
- D. Higher performing product at incumbent product price
- E. Higher performing product at higher product price

We will explore each of these pricing scenarios. Let's look at the first situation (Point A in Figure 6.1) where a potential customer is looking for *incumbent product pricing with current product performance*. (Pricing is on a sliding scale, as is performance. Current product pricing doesn't preclude negotiating a slightly different price but rather means that the price is close to the incumbent product pricing.) This first situation usually occurs in the high growth phase of a new product. After a customer verifies that the new product has marketplace acceptance, they want to avoid sales delays in the event that a supplier can't provide a key raw material. Therefore, the customer will look for a second production plant to qualify as a raw material provider – whether at their already qualified supplier or at another supplier.

The most common situation is the second one (*lower priced product with incumbent product performance*), which is represented by Point B in Figure 6.1. Most customers want the same performance that they have now, but they would like it at a lower price. As sales increase and competition comes into the market segment, there is a downward pressure on price. Customers will pass this downward price pressure onto suppliers by negotiating lower purchase prices for raw materials, as customers strive to maintain their operating margins.

FIGURE 6.1 Price Performance Grid

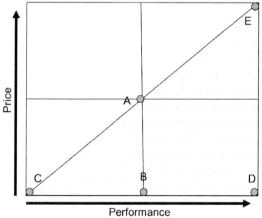

The supplier can offset some of this reduction in the selling price of its product by reducing the cost to manufacture its product. But eventually, the current technology for making a supplier's product prevents a further drop in the selling price of the product, if the supplier is to make any profit. This is represented by Box III in Figure 6.2 below. The purchase price that the customer can pay is basically equal to the supplier's cost to produce and distribute the product. Any further reduction in the selling price would cause the supplier to lose money.

At that point, the material supplier has to decide whether to continue supplying that product at a loss, look for alternate applications where customers are willing to purchase the material at higher than break-even prices, or look for a lower cost way to deliver the same or better bundle of performance properties.

Rarely will companies wait to start research until the economics reach what is shown in Box III in Figure 6.2. As a practical matter, research will usually be started when the economics have reached Box II in Figure 6.2. There is definite price compression at this point. While the supplier is still making money, the pricing trend line indicates that margins are likely to erode to unacceptable levels in the foreseeable future.

FIGURE 6.2 Marketplace Perspectives on Product Development

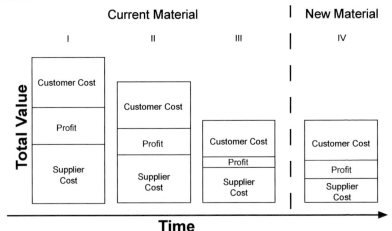

Because the driving force for developing and commercializing this lower priced product is downward price pressure from the customer, there is no room to raise the selling price of the substitute material. Therefore, this new solution will have to be made profitably at a lower cost than the current material or your management will not be interested.

Because competitors to the incumbent supplier will be working on lower cost alternatives as a way to get business at the customer, it is important for the incumbent supplier to also be working on a replacement alternative if they want to retain the business.

Sometimes there isn't a lower cost way available from the supplier to manufacture the existing product. Then the third alternative – down engineering – comes into play.

Let's look at the third situation, represented by Point C in Figure 6.1. This often occurs when the customer's new-to-the-world product has been on the market for a while. Initially, the product will be over engineered to ensure that the product can withstand in-use and delivery conditions. As the customer obtains data on product performance and returns, the customer will slowly change to lower cost and lower performing raw materials that are still appropriate for the customer's product, thus saving money.

In the fourth situation, the current raw material being used in an application will no longer work because of a change in product use requirements (e.g., longer shelf life might be needed for an emulsion). Then the customer will want *a higher performance product at the current price* as represented as Point D in Figure 6.1.

When no existing alternative works, a new product will have to be developed that meets the new performance characteristics. Developing a product that can quickly be scaled to production is critical in order to meet customers' expected demand for use in their existing product. Typically, only in production can economies of scale be reached that will allow product sales to be profitable (Figure 6.3).

The fifth situation (Point E in Figure 6.1) generally occurs in new-to-the-world applications that require *high performance*. In this case, there may be only one material that will meet the stringent requirements, resulting in a higher priced product.

FIGURE 6.3 Manufacturing Cost Curves

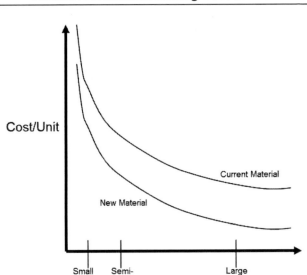

QUESTIONS TO ASK:
- Why do your customers need this product (see list on Page 28)?
- Do management and marketing at the customer's company see this as a high need?
- Does this project fit your customer's strategic direction?
- Where is this project on your customer's priority list?

7 -- How to Determine Your Customers' Product Requirements

In academic research, the specific product being made is typically well defined, especially in undergraduate laboratory experiments. This is NOT the case in commercial research. Yet you still need to determine these parameters to effectively do your research.

Sometimes the customer *will* know the exact performance standards that need to be designed into the product (e.g., a tensile strength of 1500 psi…). Other times, the customer can only tell you that the product has to pass a test they have developed as a surrogate measure for in-use performance (i.e., can't break in the "Executive Stomp" test on the final part at 23°C), which you will then have to (somehow!) translate into physical performance properties you can easily test.

Usually, you will get a combination of these two types of requirements or standards. Experienced researchers in your company will be a great resource to help translate customers' in-use performance requirements into parameters you can more easily test as you develop your product. You will prefer to have performance properties that can be measured quickly, reliably, and require little material to complete the evaluation.

It is important to understand how your product will be used in the customer's production process. Requirements for assembly, shipping, and storage are as important to a customer as final product performance because all of these factors can impact the customer's reputation and economics.

Sometimes, production processes have been optimized around the physical performance of the incumbent product, and changing from the incumbent material will require changing the production process. For example, maybe your proposed material does not stand up to the current degreasing agent the customer is using, or your material might not work in the tolerances for a snap fit tab in the customer's current assembly operations.

It is important to know whether your product is required to be a "drop-in" replacement for the current product (which is a material that can be run through the customer's existing production process - including assembly and packaging - without having to make any changes to the production process), or if the customer is willing to consider changing parts of the current process. Typically, customers will have optimized their assembly processes over the years to be as efficient and economical as possible. Therefore, they will prefer to use the existing process as much as possible even as they introduce new products into their system.

Any assembly process change during part assembly will likely mean extra costs: capital investment (for automation), rewriting procedure manuals, and retraining of key production/assembly personnel. Because many production personnel are cross-trained for multiple job responsibilities, retraining can involve quite a few people. As a result, production will usually prefer to have a "drop-in" replacement.

Your technical customer interface person will also ask the customer about use conditions that might be a weakness for your product (i.e. UV resistance, exposure to moisture) vis-à-vis the current material they are using. The customer is not as technically knowledgeable about your product as your team is, so your team will take the lead in exploring these technical issues.

For example, it is possible that while your material will be used at room temperature, it may be shipped and stored at ambient conditions. Unless otherwise specified, warehouses and railcars will have little or no heating and cooling capability. This means that your product will have to be shelf stable under some wide swings in temperature (at least -40°F to +140°F). If your product can't withstand those temperature ranges, it may have to be shipped in a climate controlled container, which will add to the shipping and storage costs of your product.

Your technical customer interface person will also get a list from the customer of all the relevant federal, state, and other government agency requirements (e.g. FDA) in the US, and in any other major countries where you expect to sell your product. This will give you a more complete picture of end product performance. Usually, your customers will be able to tell your team about the key tests and agency/government standards that relate to the applications.

You will want to know if there are any tests your material has to pass that take a long time to complete (e.g. weathering or aging studies, repeated motion endurance studies, or animal testing) so you can plan that into your development timeline. Sometimes there are shortened, accelerated tests that can be substituted for preliminary testing and evaluation. You will need to know which apply to your situation.

Your customers will often have their own corporate standards or requirements beyond the product in-use performance requirements. For example, some companies might not want any products that contain estrogen mimickers, even if they are in non-food use situations. Your technical customer interface person will again take the lead in obtaining this information.

Your customer's marketing department will be a good source for your sales organization to determine the following information:
- The geographic scope of sale for the product
- Where the customer expects to launch the product first
- In-use performance requirements
- Timing and ramp-up of product evaluation and commercialization

Your customer's production plant may also have concerns that you will have to address. A key concern is when to run trials of your product on their commercial production equipment. Each market segment has some cyclicality throughout the year. To avoid running out of stock at peak times, and avoid the need for large production equipment that may be idle at non-peak parts of the year, companies often build inventory ahead of demand.

So, for part of the year, the customer is making as much product as it can to build inventory for peak sales demand. Then production will throttle back by various amounts throughout the rest of the year.

Customers will typically allow production runs of new products when their production schedules reach their slowest point of the year. During the slower parts of the production year, the customer has more time to focus on things besides getting product out the door. For example, spring and early summer are busier production times for disposable plates and cups than is the fall.

If you meet the evaluation time window of slower production rates and your competitor doesn't, you might have an extra six months to position your company in the lead because the buildup and peak demand times can keep a plant running at high rates for several months. This extra time could potentially allow for significant sales of your product prior to your competitor's becoming qualified.

Your customer's production plant will answer these other questions about their requirements:
- Is having only one supplier production line qualified to make the product sufficient to allow commercial sales?
- If they require two sources of supply, will having two of your company's production lines qualified for providing the material suffice?
- Or do they need to have an additional supplier make the product?
- How is the customer's current product transported?

All the above questions help provide a basic framework from which to start designing a product. Consider these questions as the start of a dialogue that will lead to a detailed list of performance requirements. With your team getting answers to these questions early in the product development cycle, you can focus and accelerate your development efforts.

It's important to understand that answers to these questions aren't static. Marketplace dynamics can change or additional information may emerge that will impact the product opportunity.

It is good for your team members to periodically have follow-up dialogue with your customers. Customers may have more insight during these follow-up meetings. Also, after your team has been working on the project for a while, you may have more questions. It pays to periodically confirm that the previous answers remain valid, especially for longer term research projects.

QUESTIONS TO ASK:
- What is the geographic "scope of sale" for the product?
- What are the customer's in-use performance requirements?
- Where is the customer expecting to launch the product first?
- Does the customer require two sources of supply before they will move to commercialization?
  - if so, will having two of your company's plants qualified suffice?
  - or does the customer need to have another supplier?
- What are the transporation and storage requirements?
- What is the maximum price of the product at which the customer will consider evaluating your product?
- What does this mean for a manufacturing cost target?
- What is the timing and ramp-up schedule for product evaluation and commercialization?

8 -- How to Determine the Size of the Opportunity

Your company's management will provide your team with guidelines on the size and value of the opportunities that they are looking for. The more opportunities your project has that meet management's criteria for success, the more likely you are to get a yes vote to proceed with development. Your Project Champion will help your team understand management's criteria.

Management is challenged with the responsibility of getting the most from the dollars invested. Therefore, management will compare the risk/reward (or cost/benefit ratio) of your project with others being developed in your company. This ongoing assessment will help management determine whether to proceed with your project.

Having multiple applications where the product will work, and in areas where your company already has a customer base, will help lower the risk for your company.

Your team's marketing representative will estimate how big an opportunity the new product will be for your company. There are two aspects to size – price per unit and the number of units (volume). These two variables depend on the performance that your product can deliver and the need for that performance. Once your team has estimated both price and volume for all the targeted applications, the financial analyst on your team can calculate the value of the opportunity for your company. Most companies have standard procedures for calculating the value of each project for ease of comparing between projects.

Usually, multiple applications will be needed to provide the required profits. It is important that your team map out a plan for reaching the markets for your product. The marketing department will typically do a Market Study or Assessment to come up with the ultimate game plan. Your responsibility as a researcher will be to provide property performance information on your product and competitive products, so that marketing has a complete understanding of the scope of the potential market and competition. This requires joint communication and understanding of target market requirements.

Identifying potential opportunities for your product and developing a visual representation of these opportunities is a critical planning and communication tool. It helps Product Development Teams avoid falling into some common traps: (1) thinking of no major big project that will carry the financial load; (2) starting with a couple of small projects for a new product and getting so bogged down in those small applications that the team forgets to work toward the bigger opportunities; or (3) focusing only on a big application that will take a long time to come to fruition because of marketplace testing (e.g. automotive).

Each of these "lack of vision" traps runs the risk of your management deciding to prematurely terminate the project. In the situation where there isn't a big enough project to justify a large part of the development expense, it's hard for the project to be profitable. Each small application will tend to take so much research effort that there won't be much, if any, leverage point to gain profitability. Management will want to see a few applications of sufficient size to assure project profitability. What is considered a "major" application will vary, depending on profit potential and gross margins.

If your team is working with multiple customers in one market segment for initial qualification and sales, your team will have a detailed understanding of the required product performance for that one application. If your team selects one key customer in several target markets for the initial qualifications process, you will have a preliminary assessment on multiple market segments but not as much depth of knowledge. There is risk in either approach, and your Project Leadership Team will help clarify which strategy will be used for your product.

Some companies (e. g. the pharmaceutical industry) prefer to initially target a big opportunity (Figure 8.1) and leave the small ones for later. Others like to take a small niche and use that to work the bugs out of the product before going after the large applications (Figure 8.2).

The latter tactic can work as long as your team doesn't forget that the small target market is intended as a stepping stone rather than a final destination.

Sometimes project teams focus too much time and attention on small projects that can be early wins (Figure 8.2). They don't spend time verifying intermediate or long-term opportunities that will allow financial justification of the development project.

If your team has already listed all the potential target markets, it is less likely to get bogged down in optimizing your product for a small segment. If the concept has been tested but final customer specifications can't be met, an assessment will be made as to how much effort to expend on this application versus going after a different opportunity.

FIGURE 8.1 Large, Long Term Opportunity

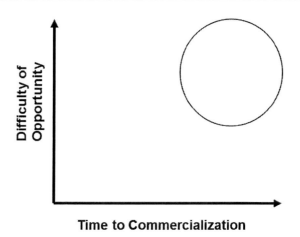

Time to Commercialization

A good decision might be to move on to another application and use the learning to make a better product for a different application. This is especially true if there is an idiosyncrasy unique to the customer's application that is keeping the product from performing well.

To make the most effective use of new products as your team develops them, it is important to target market segments where the currently developed products can be used. Leveraging each product into closely aligned market segments provides a faster return on your research. Customers see the value in using your product when applications with requirements similar to their own have had commercial success with a new product.

FIGURE 8.2 Only Short-Term Opportunities

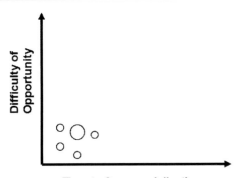

Time to Commercialization

Of course, it is best if the current applications are in the market segment of your next target customers or a highly allied field. But even if that isn't possible, the targeted customers will often understand that the performance requirements are similar in the two different applications, especially if the two applications are currently using similar products.

In fact, some industries watch the performance of new innovations in certain other industry segments because the product performance requirements are traditionally similar. For example, building and construction companies watch material performance in automotive applications, because both applications require temperature and weather extremes over long periods of time.

Having a well-articulated plan for your product introduction before the first product launch is important. This helps the team know why certain applications were chosen for initial testing of your product. If those reasons no longer hold, then the team will stop pursuing that application and work on another more promising one.

Because management likes big applications, it is easy to focus on those exclusively. If the application is one that doesn't require years of marketplace testing (such as aging studies or human testing) and can be quickly ramped up after approval, great! But it can be risky for your team to focus on only one application, such as automotive or housing, which requires extensive weathering/aging studies and then are slowly ramped up into usage (see Figure 8.1). Management may lose patience waiting that long to see profits. So also look for smaller, earlier wins with the product whenever possible (Figure 8.3).

Since the bigger applications are often farther down the development path, it is important to keep moving toward those and using these smaller applications as intermediate steps on the path to the large applications and to long-term commercial success.

This doesn't mean that one can't be successful with medical devices, drugs, automotive, or housing applications. There is a lot of money to be made there. But the reality is that initial acceptance of new technology in these applications takes longer because of the testing required to assure long-term use of the product.

Customers rarely substitute one raw material in all their applications simultaneously with another new raw material. They start with either the lowest risk or most urgent switch and will continue to switch their raw material in a controlled roll-out, always watching for in-use problems.

Therefore, migration of a new raw material to various customer product lines moves slowly once the first application is commercialized. For example, a new plastic resin might be used by a small appliance manufacturer for one part of one small appliance. After successful in-use results, the small appliance manufacturer will qualify the new resin in other parts on other small appliances at an adoption rate that makes sense for the small appliance manufacturer.

In general, your team will initially look for shorter product life applications that have shorter validation/qualification timelines and that will require volumes of material you can adequately handle, if the customer approves your product.

FIGURE 8.3 Opportunities

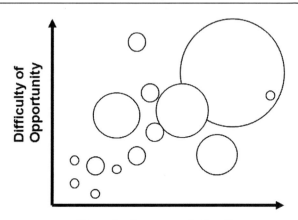

Time to Commercialization

QUESTIONS TO ASK:
- What are the set of applications that this product could be used for?
- What is the potential size of each of these opportunities and the estimated timing to develop the required product for these applications (bubble chart)?
- Is your team focused on shorter development time applications or longer term applications?
- What technical learning from one application could be applied to another application?

9 -- Why Getting Multiple Input Is Important

In any new product development project, both the supplier who is developing the product and the customer who will be using the product make commitments of significant time and resources to bring the new product to market.

Because these customers are taking a development risk, they often want an exclusive sales and development agreement for their end use application for a period of time so they can build market share.

But your company as a supplier will prefer opportunities that have broad market appeal, and not just to one customer. If your team is precluded from talking with other companies because of a development agreement with one company, you might not be getting a good market segment perspective. As a result, you could be developing a product that isn't meeting a broader market need. Or you may design the product for a unique situation of your development customer, which means you will later have to redesign the product to take it to the broader market.

Therefore, these agreements require delicate negotiations by your sales organization, because unless this one customer generates enough sales of your product, your company might not make enough profit.

While the R&D person or the purchasing agent at the customer can be a GREAT resource for you, be very careful if they are the ONLY resource for your team. Be wary of using only one person's viewpoint in designing your product, since that viewpoint might not represent either the market segment or the target company very well.

It is easy to get lulled into thinking that because the R&D person or purchasing agent your team is talking with has been in the business for decades, they ought to know what's going on, but that isn't necessarily so. There are all sorts of reasons why they might want you to bring a different product to them – and purchasing your product might not be on the list.

How frustrating and wasteful would it be to put years of research into a project just to find out the only interested party at the customer was the R&D person. Just as you as a researcher don't know all the marketplace dynamics around your product, neither does the researcher at your customer.

When a customer truly needs the product, there will usually be multi-departmental support for the product at the customer. Therefore, your team will be leery of any project where only one person in the company is giving you information and is restricting your access to other departments. Your sales organization will verify your target customer's multi-functional support. This will increase the odds that the development resources at your target customer will be available when they are needed.

Your company can't afford to spend a lot of valuable resources on something that is going nowhere with your customer. If individuals in your customer's commercial department (who are closer to the market) haven't been sold on the importance of the product, why should your company proceed with developing it?

It is vital to have the support of either the management and/or commercial organization at the customer. When neither is apparent, that should raise a big red flag.

Customers that are large companies can have lots of people who will weigh in on the decision associated with your new product. It is important for your team to know who these people are, because many of them will have the power to say no (to stop your product from being used). But there is usually just one person who has the final say (the power to say yes), and this person usually controls the funds.

The sales and marketing department at your company will take responsibility for ferreting out who those people are and understanding their criteria, in order to get a yes vote. It is important for you to know the criteria that pertain to your research and for you to work hard to meet them.

These criteria can address concerns beyond product performance. For instance, when do they intend to make their decision? When do they want to be commercial?

Once your sales representative identifies the person at the customer who can say yes to your project, that person will be a great resource in determining which of the expressed concerns need to be addressed, what are the potential show stoppers, and what is the timing for resolving issues.

Usually only a few people in your company will be in direct contact with the customer. This will help ensure that the customer receives a consistent message and also solidifies the working relationship with the customer. The salesperson is usually responsible for coordinating communication and interaction with the customer. The salesperson will also communicate any shift in interests or requirements regarding your product and stay in touch with all the key decision makers throughout the project.

We have been talking about getting multiple input from your customer. We now turn our attention to getting multiple input across the rest of the supply chain including your customer's customers, distribution, your suppliers, and others.

Trade shows are a great way to ask questions about the industry. Your team can find out from people in your target industry what their biggest business challenges are and what keeps them up at night worrying. You can find out what the latest new trends and products are in the industry. You can also learn how products that might use your new material are currently made and what these applications require. With this information your team can better create a framework and context for target applications.

Not everybody at a trade show or conference will be able to answer all these questions. But your team will develop a sense of whether there is a need for your product, whether this is a growing or shrinking opportunity, and whether you are hearing a message consistent with what your customer has been telling your team.

These conversations can give your team great insights and perspectives about technical performance needs, along with in-use conditions and concerns. Different perspectives from throughout the supply chain will help round out your understanding of how your product needs to perform.

Planning is important for getting the most out of trade shows. For example, are you prepared with key questions that need answers? Have you mapped out which booths you want to attend? Have you planned on attending the booths of key customers early so you can have a second chance to visit the booth if the person you want to talk with is on a different booth duty shift?

Major trade shows and conferences usually happen only once every one to three years. So the timing might not coincide with when your team wants the input. Don't despair. Your team members will call the relevant companies and ask them questions. Talking with distributors of your customers' products, government regulators, testing agencies, and potential customers of your customer will help complete your team's understanding of the opportunity.

It is important to understand that how you ask questions of customers can bias the responses. In the world of marketing research, there are two basic types of responses to questions: unaided and aided. An unaided response is obtained when the questioner asks a neutrally worded question. For example, "What are the top three complaints that you receive?" is an unaided question.

Aided awareness is when the questioner includes the area of interest in the question. For example, "What complaints about part leakage do you have?" is an aided question, because the question itself leads people toward an answer (part leakage rather than some other complaint), and therefore might not produce broad, unbiased information. Unaided awareness questions are best asked first, to see what issues are truly top of mind. Then you can ask probing questions about other issues. Once you have the answers to these questions, you can determine how consistent these answers are with what your developmental customer has been telling you. When your team sees inconsistencies, ask further questions.

QUESTIONS TO ASK:
- Are the requirements unique to this customer or not?
- Is there management support at the customer for this project?
- Is there multi-department support for this project at the customer?
- Who are the key decision makers at the customer and what are their key concerns?
- What is the mechanism within your team for distributing any new customer input?

10 -- How to Determine Competitive Alternatives

One way to get products to market faster is to focus on opportunities where you have the greatest chance of succeeding. This requires knowing what the competitive alternatives are. You don't want to waste time developing a product when low cost, viable alternatives are already available.

A customer will prefer to use a commercially available product if it will meet the customer's need. Not only is there history on the reproducibility of the product that the customer can review, but there is likely immediate production capacity available for making the product. This allows the customer to switch to the new raw material on their schedule, and not have to wait for the supplier to get a production plant operational.

Because time is valuable to your customers as well, they will often be exploring multiple solutions simultaneously. Since they will completely evaluate only the most promising ones, it costs them little to initially have multiple suppliers vying to provide solutions. It increases the likelihood of the customer finding the best solution.

You might think this is how the customer will be framing your alternative (Figure 10.1).

FIGURE 10.1 How You Think The Customer Is Framing Your Alternative

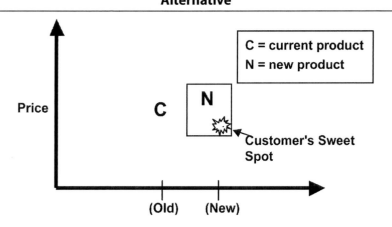

If the box around N represents the required new performance, clearly your customer's current product (C) does not fit the new requirements (N). The customer will prefer a new product to be priced at the same level, or lower, than the current product they are using, and to be at the top end of total performance (shown as Customer's Sweet Spot in Figure 10.1). (Although performance is shown as only one attribute in this chart, it is always multi-dimensional. The customer makes assessments of all these dimensions to pick the best solution.)

But your customer isn't only looking at a like-for-like replacement (e.g. polymer for polymer). Figure 10.2 shows how your customer is actually seeing the situation. They will not only be considering chemical solutions. They might also be thinking about modifying their production or shipping processes to solve the problem.

Your competition might not be another polymer manufacturer. It could be a machine shop! Your competition might not be another degreasing agent; it might be a part redesign. Think beyond chemistry solutions for potential competitors, because your customer will likely be looking at design, physics, and mechanical solutions as well.

FIGURE 10.2 How the Customer Actually Views Your Alternative

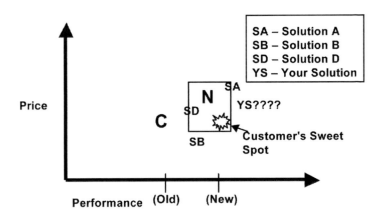

Therefore, it is important to understand what alternatives your customers are considering. This will help you position your solution versus those alternatives to determine if you have a competitive advantage. Knowing the likely alternatives and estimating the manufacturing and life cycle costs will help your team with product pricing in this application.

QUESTIONS TO ASK:
- What is the timeframe your customer has for making a decision on a solution?
- How soon before they implement the solution?
- What is the change that is driving this need?
- What will happen if your solution doesn't work (next best alternative)?
- Is this problem/solution unique to this customer?
- Who are your primary competitors and what are their competing products/solutions?
- Which solutions are serious contenders?
- Which solutions are long shots?
- What is your competitive advantage against each of these competitive products?
- Is this still an area your team wants to pursue with your new product?

11 -- How Customers Measure Cost

One key property of any product is the selling price. Your commercial organization will first determine how much a new product is worth to the customer before establishing a selling price for your product.

There are two primary ways that your product will create value for your customer: either by improving the performance of your customer's product or by lowering the cost of making their product. Your sales and marketing organization will point out your product's advantages to your customers in order to capture value.

Knowing how your product is of value to your customer, and knowing whether the customer will consider those factors in the pricing decisions, can help your team decide which opportunities to pursue first.

This requires understanding what costs and reductions in costs the customer is factoring into their equation. This is especially true in larger companies with divided accountabilities. If the business division at the customer that is making the decision does not get credit on their books for all the cost savings from any subsequent process improvement, they likely won't include it in their calculations (Figure 11.1).

FIGURE 11.1 Product Replacement Cost Calculation

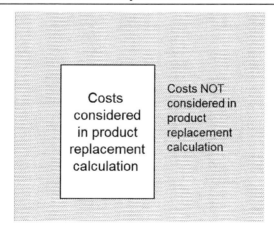

For example, if the customer is calculating cost only on the direct one-to-one raw material replacement and not the whole subassembly cost, the fact that you have eliminated an assembly processing step with your solution may not factor into your customer's calculation.

Keep in mind that the customer will usually not pay an equal increase in price for an increase in performance. After all, they have incurred costs in switching to a new product, and they want to factor in a financial incentive to themselves for switching.

Even in the case of one-for-one substitution of an equivalent competitive product, there are costs that customers might incur. For example, will retesting or recertification be required before your solution can be used?

When your product is not a like-for-like substitution, even more cost factors could be incurred. For example, will additional or special packaging or handling be needed to use your product? Will less packaging or handling be needed? Will extra processing steps be needed? Will some processing steps be eliminated? Will workers have to be trained on how to handle or use your material or solution? Is there enough available floor space in the customer's current production footprint to install your solution? Will any additional processing requirements (e.g. venting) be needed? Will some be eliminated?

Customers factor in the cost of trialing and evaluating your new product, plus the additional uncertainty of in-use performance and reliability of your product in determining the cost to use your product.

The customer will also consider risk management factors for your product or service. Is your product affecting just a minor component of your customer's product? If your product fails in-use, how big of a warranty or return issue will they have? If your product doesn't deliver in the field, how hard will it be to fix the situation? How costly?

This concern about potential field failures and the subsequent financial and image damage are risks that will decrease the value of a new product to a customer.

QUESTIONS TO ASK:
- What costs are considered in-scope for calculating current customer costs?
- In your customer's cost analysis, what savings will your solution bring?
- Will the improvements that your product brings be factored into the customer's product substitution model to provide an acceptable profit margin for this application?
- How much of a potential risk is it to the customer if your product has field failures in this application?
- How challenging are the performance requirements for this application versus what your product can easily handle?

12 -- What Is the Timing for the Decision?

When customers have a need, there is often a predetermined time attached to when they want that need filled. Therefore, it is important to understand when the customer is expecting to make a decision on an alternate solution. Typically, once such a decision is made, it will be at least a year (if ever) before the customer is willing to look at alternatives again.

The process of evaluating new raw materials can be very expensive for a customer. Therefore, once a customer decides on the raw material to use, that decision stands for many years – unless there is a compelling reason to change. Some reasons for change are: safety or warranty issues, a new technology that significantly reduces the cost for a product, an environmental concern, an economic requirement for lower cost raw material, a change in product design or performance, or a change in legal requirements.

Even if your product will give them better performance or a lower cost, they still might not look at your product immediately if you miss their evaluation window. This is especially true if the new solution is working satisfactorily.

Usually, the customer will have other issues that need attention and will focus their resources on those issues. They will wait until the next time they decide to address improving that product.

So understanding the customers' decision process and timing is important. Once your team knows the customers' decision dates, your team will develop the timeline around key customer interactions and evaluations. This timeline will help your team decide whether to pursue certain opportunities and to focus on the best opportunities for your product's success, allowing your team to more forward faster.

Let's look at the process most companies use to evaluate a new product from a supplier, which includes:

1. Initial discussion with potential suppliers
2. Running lab tests of small quantities of a supplier's material/sample to select potential candidates
3. Running larger quantities of a supplier's material on the customer's pilot facility/small production plant for further test and evaluation in-house
4. Running more material on the customer's pilot/small production plant line to make product for customer sampling to their customers
5. Running material in supplier's and customer's production plants for regulatory and customer approvals
6. Increasing production quantities as customer conversion requires

In the first step, the focus of the customer's initial discussion with suppliers is to determine what, if any, products the supplier has that will address the customer's needs and will be good candidates for the customer to evaluate. Depending on the situation, there may be non-disclosure agreements (NDAs) in place before sample quantities are shipped to the customer for testing and evaluation. These NDAs are usually done to protect the product developer's technology.

After the customer has talked with several suppliers, a number of products will be selected for initial small scale laboratory screening by the customer. These are usually simple tests that require little material yet help the customer screen out many potential choices quickly. You want your material to be part of this evaluation.

Once the selection of candidates has been reduced to just a few, the customer will then request larger amounts of material to be run on either the customer's pilot or small production line. This will allow the customer to do more tests on their finished product.

Based on these results, the customer will either decide to move forward with (at most) one to three potential solutions or to start over and look for new solutions. Up to this point, the evaluation has been mostly in-house at your customer's facility.

From here on, the expenses start to mount for your customer because they now need external interaction with their customers, regulatory agencies (to get any needed approvals), and marketing (for signoff on any product changes). They also need to work with their production facility to ensure the new product can be used safely and effectively.

Once the customer has chosen the top potential candidates, the customer will then focus on having larger sample quantities, usually 10-100 times as much material as they previously required, to make product for evaluation by their selected customers. Your customer will also evaluate the new material/product using regulatory required tests and for larger sized evaluation tests.

Let's assume your customer has determined that your material meets all the requirements. They will now want your company to demonstrate that your product can be made reproducibly on that production line. Then regulatory approval (if needed) and customer qualifications can be completed. (Typically, approval is given by a customer and regulatory agencies for a raw material that comes off a particular production line.)

Once the approvals are in place and sales contracts are signed, production officially begins. Your sales representative will determine how soon that can happen, and at what supply rate, to verify that your product can meet the customer's timeline (while also allowing for the inevitable delays in the customer's production schedule).

Although initially, your customers will allow qualification of a new product when it is made on only one production line at the supplier, they will soon want a second production facility qualified to make the new raw material. This minimizes the risk of a shortage of raw material supply due to an outage at the supplier. Either your company or a competitor will need to provide that second source of supply. Your sales organization will work with the customer to determine this.

Therefore, there are five key delivery dates for your team:
1. When customers want lab samples for preliminary evaluations
2. When customers want further material for detailed evaluation of the one to three alternatives
3. When customers want production material for pre-commercial approvals (to customers, regulatory agencies)
4. When customers want the first sales order shipped
5. When customer want to have a second source of supply approved

These are important because each alters the amount of product that your company has to supply to the customer.

To meet these five dates, your team may have to supply more than just the product. You may also have to provide:
- Pre-production trial information that the customer requires from you
- Post-production trial testing results
- Information and certifications to alternate geographies

One example of a timing misfit for a new product in development is a product that increases production throughput for a customer. Products that increase customers' production throughput are of greatest value when capacity is "tight" – meaning companies are running at or near production capacity.

This usually happens either when sales of certain products rapidly increase beyond production capacity, or when an environmental or man-made disaster occurs and production capacity is immediately impacted (for example, if a plant is out of commission). In both situations, the customer will be looking for a fast way to extend their production capacity to meet the immediate demand.

To meet this demand, your product will have to be in production. In these situations, customers can't wait until you build new capacity, even if your product will be a better solution long term, because the demand for your product is now.

QUESTIONS TO ASK:
- When do the production trials need to be completed at the customer?
- Is there any pre-production trial work that needs to be done at the customer?
- If so, what is it, what must you supply, and by when to have your product run?
- What post production testing do you and the customer need to do?
- When do those post production test results need to be completed?
- How soon after the decision is made will the switch-over to the new raw material begin?
- Over what time frame will the switch-over occur?
- Where is the initial geographic focus?

Part 3

What Internal Requirements Does Your Product Need to Meet?

13 -- Addressing the Commercial Department Needs

Until this point, we have focused on external requirements for your product. In the next several chapters, we will discuss your own company's concerns and requirements that your team will have to address. This chapter focuses on your commercial organization's needs.

Many companies manage their business from a strategic perspective, which provides the fundamental focus for all parts of the business. Your commercial organization is focused on establishing connections with the key target segments and customers, consistent with your company's strategy. These relationships help the commercial organization understand the needs of these customers and identify opportunities for sales of your company's current and future products.

Establishing these working relationships takes time – maybe as many as seven or more interactions with a prospective customer before a buying situation is established. As a result, most of the commercial organization's time is focused on the strategic customers in the key market segments.

Your development team will likely make headway faster where your organization is already a known and respected supplier, all things being equal. A new segment will take extra time and work to penetrate. Therefore, developing products for a core segment is an easier sell.

The most difficult situation is a market segment where your company has a negative reputation. This can happen for a variety of reasons. Perhaps your company stopped making a product that the market segment wanted, or maybe your company has submitted lots of products to this segment in the past but had no sales.

Therefore, developing a product for market segments and customers with a strong strategic fit for your company is very important to the commercial organization.

Your marketing and sales group will assess the marketplace dynamics for your team. They will determine if there is a need for your product in the market. If there is a need, they will help bracket the sources of value to the customer and develop an estimate of the pricing that is likely to be possible for each application.

They will also help your team understand who the competitors are, what barriers to entry there might be for your product, and what the competitive alternatives are for your product. They will also help your team identify potential development partners; some companies are just easier to work with than others for developmental activities.

Marketing will determine the initial geographic focus for the early stage product development. Depending on availability of commercial resources in that geography to help your team, this may accelerate or delay your development activities.

Your project's financial analyst will use the above information as input to determine the profitability of your project and whether that profitability will meet the strategic hurdle rates for development projects in your organization.

The amount of time your commercial organization has available to advance your product is going to be impacted by the number of strategic initiatives they are currently being asked to implement. Sometimes several corporate initiatives require simultaneous attention, and sometimes your commercial organization might be in the midst of a big company launch of another product for the next few months. In both cases, you can expect that they will have limited capacity for other projects or initiatives.

QUESTIONS TO ADDRESS:
- How strongly does this product fit the strategic direction of your company?
- Are any of your company's strategic customers development candidates for your product?
- What materials and how much are likely to be used in this product?
- How is your product competitively advantaged versus alternatives?

14 -- Addressing the Needs of Production and Shipping

One of the biggest internal barriers you will face as a researcher is getting the semi-plant or production plant engineers to scale up your lab process.

The first priority of production engineers is the safe running of their production equipment. When in doubt, an engineer will err on the side of caution and vote "no" to running an experiment. By spending time with the production engineer, the two of you can work toward a mutually positive solution and experience.

This extra discussion time will not only result in a better and lower cost product for your company but also fewer experiments. Factoring in the production design limitations early in the development process can save you a lot of frustration and scrambling later, as well as ensure that you are developing a scalable product.

Discuss your proposed solution with the plant engineers and understand where there might be "pinch points" from a production standpoint. Solicit their ideas on what might work and what definitely isn't going to work in the plant. Understanding these limitations can be as important as your customers' requirements.

Some common topics around production limitations are:
- Equipment materials of construction
- Heat exchange rates
- Agitation rates and dead spots
- Pumping rates
- Transfer speeds and shear rates
- Maximum operating pressures
- Viscosity, and
- Exothermic and endothermic reactions

Much of this information can be exchanged in only a few hours of discussion.

Here is a brief discussion of two key scale-up parameters: surface-to-volume ratio and mixing. Because the surface-to-volume ratio of a production vessel is smaller than a lab reactor, there are scale parameters to consider in designing your lab experiments. A larger amount of heat has to be exchanged (added to or removed from the production vessel) in a production scale reactor than in a lab reactor, and there is a lower surface-to-volume ratio of a production reactor. This combination of factors means that heat is exchanged more slowly in a production reactor than in a lab reactor.

Therefore, the rate of addition of chemicals will sometimes have to be slowed in production to allow heat to be transferred without destroying the product. Uniform mixing will also occur at a slower rate in a production vessel due to the volume of material that has to be mixed. Understanding these and other parameters, and designing a product in the lab that will likely meet production equipment requirements, can go a long way toward speeding up commercialization of your product.

For example, it is quite easy to put a 20 ml shot into a one gallon reactor in less than three seconds, with 100 rpm agitator speed for fast mixing of a low viscosity liquid. It is quite another thing to disperse 70 liters in the same amount of time and get good mixing in a 3500 gallon reactor!

Additional concerns specific to your project should also be discussed. You will develop experiments to address these production scale-up issues and place them on the Project Plan timeline. These will also become the focus of future discussion between you and production as the project moves forward.

Plan to address these key issues early in the development process while you have time to think through and do something about them. Not addressing these key issues will likely extend your project timeline.

By looking at other lab products that have been scaled previously in the production equipment you expect to use, you can get a feel for the various scale ratios. But not every factor may be known. So it is important to address ahead of time as many that *are* known and then discuss with a production engineer the unknown scale factors to get an estimate of how to scale from the laboratory level. You may be required to run experiments that will bracket the change in performance with changes in the product recipe to assure manufacturing that the product can be safely made in the production plant without setting up or destroying any of the production equipment.

Usually the initial scale-up will be done in a slightly smaller commercial reactor that may be older. Make sure you understand any differences between this initial trial reactor and a full-scale production one.

Because production plants are so critical to the ongoing success of your company and the ramifications of negative consequences to the equipment are so much greater, most companies require a pre-production safety review before agreeing to run a new product in a production plant.

These safety review teams usually include knowledgeable manufacturing, research, and risk assessment individuals who are not part of the project that is being reviewed. These safety reviews will outline any activities (whether in production or in the lab) that need to be completed before the new product can be run in the larger scale vessel.

Modifications to existing equipment may be needed to make your product successfully. Your early and continuous discussions with production engineering should ensure that the needed equipment is ready to go, including necessary modifications, without delaying the scale-up process.

Periodically update the production engineer about your results. The engineer might determine further production constraints or considerations for you to address.

Your support in getting any extra equipment for production scale-up will be greatly appreciated by production engineers. Especially in tough economic times, the amount of money available for capital spending is tight to non-existent. So it can be hard to free up dollars for a new pump or tank or whatever is needed. Usually, in large companies the production plant can find most of the needed equipment in the production "bone yards" where surplus equipment is stored. Talk with your production engineer about how you can support the effort to get the extra equipment needed to do the scale-up right and minimize production issues down the road.

You want to avoid having the plant operators make production swap-outs on-the-fly. If something needs to be changed out on a tight timeline, it will likely start just at operator shift change, which will delay the process. Then you won't know whether it was the time delay or some other factor that altered the expected results. Make every production run count – plan ahead.

Breaking into a production schedule to make an experimental run when a plant is running at full capacity is *very* expensive because sales of the current product are guaranteed. When a production plant is running "flat out" (meaning at full capacity) just to keep up with customer orders, only a crisis at a number one customer is going to allow a trial run of a new product in the production plant – and the decision to break into the production schedule will be made by the top business manager! Therefore, determine when cyclical production slow times are likely to occur and prepare to schedule your production experiments then.

What types of materials are your production plant used to handling – solids, liquids, or gases? Whichever ones they currently handle, they will have equipment in place and will be familiar with how to handle them. Therefore, as you develop your product, think carefully about the components of your product and whether they are in a form that the plant is already capable of handling.

People feel more comfortable doing what they are already doing. This applies to your production plants as well. If they are used to routinely handling only liquids, be wary of any solutions that now require them to handle powders (or vice versa). Yes, lots of plants are proficient at handling powders, but it doesn't matter if your plant isn't one of them.

If you ask your production plant to run a new form of raw material, they will likely have to install new feed tanks, new delivery equipment, new safety protection, new storage containers, and conduct extra/new safety training for operators. All of this is extra work – and potential risk – for the plant.

Another concern production plant engineers have about any new raw material is cross-contamination of their other products. The efficient running of a production plant requires minimal changes from one product to another in the same production vessel. This minimizes cleanout time, which is production downtime. This becomes especially burdensome in production plants that run on a continuous basis. They react raw materials and produce off-spec material while they wait for the system to stabilize within the production specification for the next product.

If there is the possibility of a negative reaction or product contamination from the introduction of any new raw material, manufacturing may have to revise the production sequence in order to accommodate the new product. This is another cost factor that will have to be considered when determining the overall economics of the new product.

There are shipping standards for materials, including the safe loading and unloading. The production plant will need to determine how to safely receive and ship your materials (raw materials and end product). The closer your shipping requirements are to their normal operations, the easier it will be for production.

With the prevalence of just-in-time inventorying of raw materials, it is important to work with the production plant to address any inventory holding concerns for raw materials for your new product. Some potential concerns include: (1) does the plant have adequate warehousing space? (2) Are there special storage conditions for any new raw materials that you might be using versus what is routinely used in your production plant?

For a new product to be successful, it is important that there be a big enough aggregated demand to enable a company to make the product profitably. If your new product can be made in an existing production facility, the risk of market acceptance will be less for your company (from a capital standpoint) than if a whole new plant is required. Therefore, it is important to determine where the product is likely to be made. Once the manufacturing plant is identified, the volume of product needed for economic viability can be determined.

As you can see, what appear to be small changes in the laboratory can have huge implications when addressed at production plant scale. This is why so much time can be lost if you are not in communication with production engineers in the earliest stages of the research.

At some point you and the production engineer will have to develop and implement a plan for evaluation of a primary and secondary source of supply of any new material that is needed to make your product. Your production engineer and supply chain manager can help you with this, including the timing for the evaluations.

Your team members who are interacting with customers will inform production of any industry tests that must be performed on your new product before release to customers. This will enable the production plant to provide the information that customers expect to receive with each shipment. Your research group may also be involved in helping production set up any new quality control testing that production needs to monitor product quality before release to customers.

QUESTIONS TO ASK:
- What is the currently proposed manufacturing process?
- What changes in the manufacturing process could significantly lower the cost to manufacture?
- Where are there "pinch points" for the production of your product?
- What new raw materials will you be asking production to use?
- What changes will be needed in production to use any new material you will introduce?
- Are there any special storage conditions for the new raw materials?
- Will your new product be able to be made on existing production equipment?
- What modifications will be needed?
- Does the production plant have adequate warehousing space?
- Do you need to address shipping concerns?
- What is the minimum production volume your product has to generate to be a viable possibility?
- What new tests will production have to perform?

15 -- What Requirements Does Research Have?

Research strives to develop products that meet the needs of current and future customers. Products are developed by applying relevant knowledge and insights to advance development and commercialization. Companies hope to do this at the lowest possible cost.

The research department has its own set of concerns that need to be addressed. One of the first areas is whether your technical solution is an area of technology in which your company has already amassed a lot of knowledge.

More fundamental research will be required to gain a solid grasp of any new area of technology and this will extend the timeline for the project.

Research will require a rigorous identification of the competitive alternatives, assessment of the competitive strengths and weaknesses of your technology versus competitors in the targeted applications, assessment of the legal freedom to practice (patents) and the ability to protect the technology area needed for your product.

An initial technology assessment will help R&D management determine whether your company can maintain a technical competitive advantage, should you develop a product that meets marketplace needs.

There are two primary technical ways that companies sustain a competitive advantage – patents and trade secrets. The more patents that a company can obtain in an area of technical research, the stronger its position is likely to be in that segment. Intellectual property is discussed in detail in Chapter 20 – How to Protect What You Have Developed.

The more knowledge and experience a company has in an area of technology, the faster it can solve any problems that arise in research, scale-up, or customer trials. All of this helps improve a company's competitive technical advantage.

The research department will also assess whether new development equipment will be needed to run experiments at the lab scale and whether new testing and analysis procedures will need to be developed and verified. Both of these things can add time to the Project Development timeline.

Research will want an assessment of the chemicals that will be used in your product. Companies have guidelines that they won't use certain chemicals in their processes. Your supervisor will be able to provide that information to you.

There are a variety of reasons why companies won't use certain chemicals. It might be because their equipment and facilities are not adequately equipped to handle the materials, or because it is very expensive for them to handle them, or because they have a policy of using only GRAS (generally recognized as safe) materials because they are primarily a supplier to food use applications and don't want to have concerns about any cross-contamination in their plants.

Your research group will be required to provide estimates of raw materials to be used, a production process, and safe handling requirements to help the financial analyst estimate manufacturing costs.

QUESTIONS TO ASK:
- What information is already available in this technology area?
- Has your company developed and scaled up a similar product from the lab to production?
- What patents are already in this area of technology?
- Which ones does your company have?
- Which are owned by others?
- Are there chemicals that won't be allowed for use?
- Can this product be developed on existing laboratory equipment?
- Do new testing procedures need to be developed in order to participate in this opportunity?

16 -- What Are The Environmental, Safety, Ethical, Societal, Regulatory, and Legal Requirements?

Government and non-government agencies can influence activities in the market segments that your team is targeting.

These agencies issue standards and guidelines, which are designed to protect the safety and health of consumers, workers, and the communities in which they reside during manufacture, transportation, and use of products. These standards and guidelines include such common ones as American Society for Testing and Materials (ASTM) standards, Food & Drug Administration (FDA) requirements, and Good Manufacturing Practices (GMP) for manufacturing and testing of pharmaceuticals.

All of these guidelines and more are designed to prevent adverse reactions. Many of the guidelines that have been established are based on previous testing or experience.

Review and follow these requirements. Your company will also have policies, procedures, and guidelines in place to prevent accidents from occurring. Learn and abide by those, too.

Because many chemicals are handled in highly concentrated form and can have significant negative consequences for humans if handled incorrectly, there is tight regulatory control of the industry – in manufacturing, delivering, and using the materials.

The chemical industry must comply with environmental, health, and safety compliance regulations designed to address the safe use of chemicals and plastics – both for workers and for end users. All products must be shipped with Material Safety Data Sheets (MSDS) describing the safe handling and storage of liquids, powders, and gases, for example. Some chemicals can be dust hazards, some are lachrymators, and some are pyrophoric. The Food & Drug Administration (FDA) has written guidance about the safe use of chemicals (www.fda.gov).

The government rules and regulations for shipping and using hazardous chemicals include use of Material Safety Data Sheets (MSDS) and labeling of products to inform users and shippers of how to safely handle your product. An MSDS explains the hazards associated with the product, as well as what precautions to take to avoid those hazards.

There are government standards that address the amount of airborne or waterborne particulates that can be released – both in short-term bursts and over longer time frames. If your production plant is already running at or near the allowable exposure or release limit of an airborne or waterborne substance that will be part of your new product, there may be some pushback by production. It is important to be sensitive to these issues. Excursions above the stated limits in a permit can cause a plant to be shut down until a remedy is installed. There may also be fines involved. On the other hand, if your product has less of a molecule that is near an airborne or waterborne limit, that can be a good thing.

More and more companies are addressing the total life cycle cost of the products that they produce. You want to think through whether there are any issues with disposal of your product after its useful life. Will your company have to set up a reclamation service to handle the safe disposal of parts containing your product?

With the renewed interest globally in the environment, many companies currently are favoring green products. How each company addresses this will vary. One company might be interested in developing products that improve our environment (for example, to use in solar power), another in lowering energy usage to reduce its carbon footprint, or in using materials (or developing products) that are more environmentally friendly (total life cycle costs).

Most consumers are increasingly demanding "greener" products. It will be important to know how your proposed product compares to existing products from a green standpoint.

Being green is just one type of social requirement. Others might be sourcing locally, sourcing from small businesses, sourcing from women-or minority-owned businesses, or sourcing from veteran-owned businesses. Other types of social requirements might be the key market segments to target: medical, agriculture, pharmaceutical, water purification, alternative energy, and other areas that improve the quality of human life.

In the US, when things go wrong with a product post-purchase, there is a tendency to sue someone – anyone – to recover damages. Therefore, lawyers will seek out which companies have "touched" the product that didn't deliver sufficient performance, and then attach those companies' names to the lawsuit. Lawyers are especially looking for companies with "deep pockets" (those that have lots of money) as a place to get remuneration.

One way your team can minimize any in-use difficulties with your product is to assess what issues might occur (risk assessment) and then determine how you can develop your product or delivery of your product to prevent those situations from arising. Your legal department will help you assess these potential warranty and liability issues.

What issues can occur *after* the product is shipped to the customer? If an incorrect use of your product causes problems, will your company be held liable? Usually, if the product is being used in a controlled environment (e.g. by another chemical company) in their process, problems don't arise because established procedures will be monitored and followed to prevent problems.

However, if your product is being applied by multiple small users with varying degrees of knowledge and experience (e.g. construction contractors), the amount used and procedures followed for an application can vary widely, leading to possibly poor results and/or handling problems.

An example of a potential problem: assume your material is used in a small component that is inside a larger and more expensive assembly; if the small part fails and the larger assembly is no longer usable, will your company be held liable? What could the financial exposure be? What is the probability of this occurring?

That doesn't mean that there will never be a lawsuit, even if you do everything correctly. But it does minimize problems and provides your company with protection from paying large claims needlessly.

All forward thinking companies are concerned about maintaining the health and safety of their employees – both now and in the future. Therefore, chemical companies not only provide protective equipment for their employees and safety training, they also adjust the R&D and production environments to reduce the likelihood of worker exposure to hazardous materials during daily operations.

Depending on what products your company is currently making in its production plant and what materials your product may be adding to the mix, changes to the production equipment may be needed to ensure the safety of workers and surrounding communities. These changes and their costs will be factored into product commercialization costs.

Companies typically have policies about behaving ethically. This includes things such as not taking kickbacks or not paying bribes to get business. One aspect of ethical behavior that will impact you the scientist includes not over promising on what the product can deliver or the timetable for R&D development. Sometimes in the drive to get a piece of business, a scientist can be too optimistic on estimating the development schedule. The multi-functional Project Plan should reflect realistic timing for developing R&D products.

QUESTIONS TO ASK:
- Are there issues with the safe disposal of your product after its useful life?
- Are there any water or air permit issues with the use of the raw materials used in the manufacture of your new product?
- Have you provided realistic estimates into the Project Plan for completing your research?
- What information do you need to factor into your research as a result of the risk assessment?
- Are there any difficulties in the use of your product that might cause the customer's product to not perform properly?
  - What would be the likely consequences?
  - What can your company do to prevent them?

Part 4

How Do You Effectively Get Your Solution Developed and Produced?

17 -- How to Get Started and Go Faster

Unlike undergraduate science classes in which experiments were nicely laid out, industrial research doesn't have such a clear path. It is your responsibility to determine what information is needed to make the desired product reproducibly.

Doing experiments is usually the longest and most expensive way to gain knowledge. Therefore, run experiments only when the information isn't available to you through other means. This chapter will help you determine where to begin your initial experiments and how to increase the rate of progress in subsequent experiments.

First, understand the desired performance characteristics of the product you are trying to develop. You can obtain this information from your Project Team commercial members. Although the requirements might not initially be as narrowly defined as they ultimately will be, you should still be able to begin your research.

Second, determine the general area of technology that you will explore to find a solution, the production equipment and process, and the development timeframe. Then start filling in the knowledge and experience of others to determine how much is already known. To reduce your research time, begin your initial experiments as close to your final product as possible.

Consider it to be a giant puzzle. First, develop the big picture of what you are trying to create, fill in all the known pieces, and then tackle the unknown pieces. Part of the project itself is determining what you can use or re-purpose for your needs.

Building on what is known can save you significant amounts of time and money. Not only do you have a starting point that is closer to your end goal, but you have a body of knowledge you can read and explore to give you a feel for developing your final product faster (Figure 17.1). "Urban legend" suggests that for every hour spent in learning, preparing, and planning for a project, 7-10 hours of doing can be saved.

Figure 17.1 Starting As Close to the End As Possible

"New to you" is not the same as "new to your company." Often a company will work in an area of research several times before all the pieces are available for commercial success. Learn what previous research has been conducted by your company in this area.

Look at all the internal resources your company has. This includes discussions with researchers, reading data books, research reports, and internal presentations. Not all the knowledge that you need will be in an easily searchable form. Some things you will discover only by asking questions, whether because it was never written down, or it may be in someone's research notebook and not available in a searchable database.

Experienced scientists can give you information that will help direct your next experiments and give you a feel for the magnitude of the changes that you can make without seriously affecting any equipment.

Learn what you can from products or solutions that are similar to what you are attempting to make. When a similar product is something that has been made by your company, find the researchers who worked on the project, read the reports, then ask the researcher any additional questions. You will be surprised at what a few days of dedicated searching can produce.

Even if what you are attempting to make has a unique set of properties that are not yet commercially available, there are still products that will be similar in characteristics to what you are trying to develop. Even with new-to-the-world products and technology, much of the technology in those products is already known (the 80/20 rule). It is just reapplied to a new situation, and most of the research is focused on overcoming the hurdles in the truly new parts.

After you have completed your internal search for help, it is time to look externally. Common sources of information include published research, proceedings, and papers from scientific conferences, trade shows, academics working in the field, research consultants in your area of technology, and published books and patents.

When you start doing research in a new area, you always want to do a patent search. You want to ensure that you are "free to practice" any new technology you are targeting to develop, or application that you are focusing on, and to determine if you can protect any truly new and novel technology for your company that you may develop. Your company's patent attorney will help you with this.

You want to initially do a broad search in the material science in which you are interested and in the end use applications you will likely be pursuing. You might also want to look at process patents. A broad initial search will help you find any areas where your company might be precluded from developing your products.

The authors of patents can only claim something that is novel. In order to demonstrate that novelty, the authors must first articulate the relevant information about what is already known to those "skilled in the art." They might include recipes for making different products or show combinations of molecular properties that yield desired physical performance properties.

By reading patents for these details, the information that is known to those "skilled in the art" becomes known to you also. You can use this as key basic information upon which to build your understanding of an area of technology. You can also use the names of the patent authors and referenced patents to do further literature searching.

These patented products can be a great resource in bracketing your research. At no point do you want to develop a product that infringes on an existing patent without first obtaining a license from the patent owner to use the patent.

Don't be discouraged if you don't have all your experiments mapped out at the start. Commercial research has many unknowns. Do those experiments first that are most likely to move you forward quickly. As you progress on your project, new ideas and experiments will become clear to you.

If you want to get to the end result faster, it is important to make significant changes in your product's recipe/formulation when going from one experiment to the next. Don't be afraid to make 10-50% adjustments in a product ingredient in a single experiment. That doesn't mean that every experiment will be a large change, only that you should always think in terms of how big of a change you can make with each experiment.

For example, if the surfactant level ultimately needs to be increased by 20% from where your current formulation is, increasing it in 0.5% increments will take you 40 experiments. But if you change it in 10% increments; you will need only two experiments. This will save you probably two months of research time. That savings is for just one variable, and you will have multiple variables to explore with your product. By simply increasing the increments from experiment to experiment, you can save yourself years of experimenting. Smaller changes are great when you are fine tuning a final product formulation.

Knowing which variables can be changed in large increments without significantly destroying the product and which properties to change in smaller increments will allow you to make the fewest number of experiments.

As an intermediate goal, focus on developing a "stable system" that will not crash your equipment. Then work on changes in your product that will meet the desired performance.

An experimental design algorithm is one of the fastest ways to figure out which experiments to run. The algorithm uses information from previous experiments and knowledge to create a model for determining the impact of changes in product ingredients and operating conditions on product properties. The computer program determines experiments to consider running next, based on the algorithm and your desired product properties.

If you are fortunate enough to have a databank of experimental results and an algorithm to work with, you should be able to quickly hone in on some good starting points. Even if the algorithm isn't a perfect match for what you are trying to do, use its best estimate as a starting point and go from there. As more experimental results are input into the databank, the predictive capability of the model will improve.

If you don't have an algorithm to use, you'll need to estimate a starting point using the knowledge of other experienced researchers plus your own experience and knowledge. Don't be discouraged if progress is slow at first. There will be experiments that can teach you something but may not move the product performance closer to the end goal. Take time to learn from those experiments, and figure out how to modify what you know about making the desired product.

Unexpected results can be a source of new discovery and information. Talk it over with other scientists, because these may be new findings which can have patent implications and commercial impact on current or future products. Even if you don't have time to follow up today on the unexpected findings, it may be research you or another colleague can do later.

As you develop further information during the project, others may have additional knowledge that will be useful. So keep key people in your company in the loop about progress on your project through periodic discussions.

QUESTIONS TO ASK:

- What work has already been done in this area – both internally and externally?
- Who can you talk with about past work in this area?
- How can you get a patent search done?
- What patents deal with research on various aspects of your project?
- Will your company be "free to practice" the targeted technology you are trying to develop?
- What information can be used to complete your project faster?
- Are you clear on where you will require new research?
- Are there any experts in, or close to, your "unknown waters" that you can talk with to get a better understanding for the area?
- How can you get the most information from a conference?
- What experiments should you do first?
- Where can you make bigger changes in your product recipe/ formulation that will help you move the project forward faster?
- Is anything likely to blow up, seize up, or shut down as a result of this degree of experimental change?
- Who can you talk with to help decide how much of a change in a recipe you can reasonably make?

18 -- How to Use Meetings Effectively

When you are in charge of a meeting, keep it as brief as possible, on task, send an agenda ahead of time, and above all else, start and end on time. The shorter you keep the meetings and the more on task you keep them, the greater the likelihood that people will attend and that decisions will get made.

Be clear in the agenda as to what decisions are to be made during a meeting so people can come prepared. Have the Project Plan updated before meetings so valuable meeting time isn't taken up just noting work that has been done.

Attendees should have a chance to review data before the meeting. Then the meeting can be used to iron out details, have needed discussions to keep the project on track, and make decisions quickly.

One of the major slowdowns in a project timeline is waiting for meetings to occur, especially those for stage gates and other major decisions. The tendency is for teams to schedule the decision meeting after all the necessary information is collected, rather than estimating ahead as to when the information will be available.

Typically, it takes three to four weeks to get together a group of four or more people in a large company to have a meeting of an hour or more, especially if management is involved. The longer the meeting and the more people involved, the longer it usually takes to schedule.

This includes stage gate reviews and production pre-startup inspections. So factor in that time lag when you start scheduling any meetings. This time lag creates no value as the team waits for a determination from management whether to move the project to the next stage of development.

If you are going to have meetings on a regular basis, set up the schedule for several months in advance so the meeting times will be blocked out on people's calendars. If you have a global team, be aware of particular holidays in other countries, along with time zone differences.

Once you have scheduled a meeting, you need to prepare for it. You want to have all the information available for making decisions at the meeting so the decision won't be delayed or postponed to yet another meeting.

There are several things you can do to increase the likelihood that a decision will be made at the first meeting: create an agenda, and send it out a week in advance – if possible, along with all supporting materials/pre-read information, or a link to the information.

With the advances in technology it isn't necessary for people to always meet in the same room. But it does require that participants who are meeting through their computer avoid doing other work, rather than participating in the meeting. Keeping meetings short and on task can help participants stay focused on the meeting, not e-mail or other distractions. Learn the latest tools that your company offers to run remote meetings effectively.

Make presentation of your information as clear and crisp as possible. When it comes to slides, it is best to think simple and elegant, rather than elaborate. Focus only on the key aspects and then add the extra information verbally.

QUESTIONS TO ASK:
- What tools does your company have for running meetings remotely?
- Does your group have a standard template for meeting agendas?
- Are you prepared before attending each meeting?

19 -- How to Get Ad-Hoc Member Participation

Some team members will be assigned to your project full time and others will be involved only periodically. Usually these part-time people have an expertise that is needed for only short periods.

These ad-hoc team members usually have multiple projects competing for their time and expertise. If there is someone whose help you will need, talk with that person before you need the services about when you will need help and why. The ad-hoc member can then estimate how much time will be required and what information will be needed from you in advance to help him or her do the job better and faster.

By providing each ad-hoc member what he or she needs and in a timely fashion, you are making that person's life easier. Anything that you can do to minimize the amount of time that ad-hoc individuals need to work on your project will increase the odds that they will help you in a timely manner.

As your timeline and requirements change, keep these ad-hoc members updated on when their help will be needed. Because you have spent time upfront helping them understand the project, they may be able to contribute in additional ways beyond your original expectations.

If you have a situation where you aren't getting the ad-hoc resources that were committed or the resources aren't being provided in a timely manner, it is usually because of conflicting priorities. When the resources aren't available as promised, you can get help from either your direct supervisor, or team leader, or both. Work with them to determine next steps.

It's also good to give thanks and recognition for the help of others beyond your team as you move forward on your project. Nothing can set your project apart as quickly as thanking people for their help. It makes a human connection in an increasingly depersonalized world.

It also goes a long way in getting people not assigned to your project to help occasionally. You will stand out among your peers because so many people fail to thank and recognize others. As an added bonus, people will be more forthcoming in helping you next time if their efforts are recognized this time. We all want to know that someone recognizes our efforts at a human level, not just with a paycheck.

Many companies have a process in place to recognize people and teams. They also have funds set aside for reward and recognition programs. Know how much funding is available and the criteria for using the funds. Your Human Resource person or your supervisor can answer these questions for the team. If you are not familiar with how to use the system, get training.

Your team will likely establish general criteria to use on your project for celebrating success. People often think that recognition is "hokey" – until they are the recipient! It always feels good to the recipient. Even people who are shy appreciate a sincere thank you. Just be mindful of each person's preferences for the manner of receiving thanks.

Often teams will celebrate when they meet major milestones or complete a stage gate. This keeps people motivated and increases the team spirit. You help your team when you take advantage of opportunities to recognize your team members for their contributions.

If your team doesn't have a recognition or celebration program in place, talk with the project manager and request such a program. You can then start proposing people and situations to recognize. Once the program is started, others will join in and participate, as they enjoy getting the recognition themselves.

Think in terms of small dollar amounts for recognition of actions that help move the project forward in small ways. It could be a pizza, a large cookie cake, a box of donuts, a special pen, a cap, or a jacket. Even an E-card has value. You can write thank you letters outlining what people did to help move your project forward and thank them for their efforts (be sure to copy their supervisor). The important thing is that people know the *reason* for the recognition, and that all involved are given a few moments to celebrate.

QUESTIONS TO ASK:
- What information can you provide to ad-hoc members to minimize the amount of time they need to spend on your project?
- What can you do to get an ad-hoc member to meet your timeline?
- Have you thanked those that have helped you?
- Have you recognized their contributions?
- What company mechanisms are in place that you can use to recognize others who have helped with your project?
- What are your company guidelines for recognition?

20 -- How to Protect What You Have Developed

All researchers want to ensure that their new discoveries are protected from use by competitors. This not only helps protect your company's competitive advantage, it also provides a platform for future growth.

There are two primary ways that companies protect their intellectual property: patents and trade secrets. It is important to determine as soon as possible which path you will take with your technology, based on the advice of your team's patent attorney (Figure 20.1).

1. Will your proposed technical solution infringe on anyone's existing patent?
2. If yes, should you consider acquiring/licensing the right to that technology? Or should you look for an alternative technology?
3. If it doesn't infringe on an existing patent, is this a technology that your company should consider patenting or keeping as a trade secret?

Assuming you go the patent route, your team will also want to determine in which areas of the world you will need patent coverage. In some countries, the patent application has to be filed <u>before</u> any public disclosure. In others, you have a time period after the initial public disclosure to file. In some countries, the decision on who gets a patent is based on the first to <u>file</u>. In other countries it is the first to <u>invent</u>.

FIGURE 20.1 Technology Decision Tree

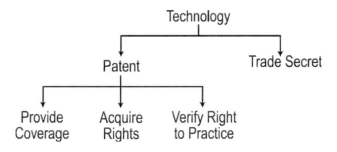

Because of the complexity of patent law, it is good to have discussions early with your patent attorney. This will give you time to uncover all relevant patents and put together an assessment of your company's ability and limitations to produce the proposed technical solution. You and your patent attorney will also develop a Technology Protection Map and strategy early in the project.

Some aspects of the patent strategy include: are you going for one extensive and encompassing patent, for process patents, or application patents? These discussions will impact support experiments you'll need to do and the timing for writing patent applications.

The Unites States Patent and Trademark Office (USPTO) website (www.uspto.gov) is an excellent resource. The Patent Office examines applications and grants patents when appropriate. The USPTO is also the location for forms and regulations for filing an international application under the Patent Cooperation Treaty (PCT). Your patent attorney will assist you with filing a PCT.

The USPTO gives inventors the opportunity to file provisional patents, which establish effective filing dates without having to provide all the support information for a full patent application. This gives researchers a 12-month window to compile the rest of the information needed for a patent application. If the full patent isn't filed within 12 months, the earlier established date with the provisional filing is no longer in effect. Your patent attorney will help you decide when to file for a provisional patent application.

Consult with your patent attorney to determine if a secrecy agreement is needed with customers. An appropriate legal document can be drafted which will protect your company's interests. Usually attorneys work with standardized agreements which have been previously vetted internally in your company.

Even then, secrecy/non-analysis agreements can take months to get all parties to reach agreement and sign. Properly executed secrecy/

non-analysis agreements with the customer should prevent reverse engineering and unwanted access to your product. It is important that your project team understands your company's policy and requirements around these factors before talking with or sampling any product or prototypes to vendors, customers, or contract manufacturers.

If your company decides not to apply for patents, trade secrets may still be a possibility. A trade secret is any information – such as a formula, device, program, process, method, or technique – which provides the owner with economic value and which the owner works to keep a secret.

Trade secrets are used when something could be easily modified with almost the same results if it were known and when the information can't be easily reversed engineered from the product that is being sold. Trade secrets are protected by not divulging them outside of your organization.

Your company may need to negotiate a license to an existing patent in order to practice your new technology. This will usually be done in the early stages of R&D for two reasons.

First, the lack of such a license will be considered a "show stopper" for the project and would need to be negotiated before a significant amount of development dollars are spent.

Second, the economic outcome to your company of the new technology isn't as well known early on, so the owner of an existing patent won't have as much leverage in the negotiations.

Any information that becomes public knowledge, no matter who in your company relayed the information, could hurt your chances of getting a patent and decrease the value of a trade secret. Therefore, get legal clearance for any presentations about your technology outside your company, including any meetings with potential customers and technical conference presentations.

Most companies have a process for signoff on presentations or reports before they are available for external use. What you and others say in non-scripted situations also requires your vigilance in not giving away important proprietary information.

In some specific cases, public disclosure may be the preferred tactic of ensuring that you, and others, can practice your new technology because once information is publicly disclosed, no one can patent it. Usually, if this tactic is used, the publication will occur in some obscure journal, which can then later be brought to light if a competitor decides to file for a patent.

QUESTIONS TO ASK:
- Is it best for your company to apply for patents or keep this technology a trade secret?
- If you are going the patent route, what is your patent strategy?
- What communication/non-analysis procedures do you have in place to make sure that trade secrets or other key confidential information are not communicated to customers or suppliers?
- Have you and your research team created a Technology Protection Map?

21 -- How to Stay Motivated

Keeping the momentum going on a long project is critical. It requires maintaining a day-to-day sense of urgency about completing work. Factors that typically keep an externally based sense of urgency in front of us – management attention and customer commitments – just aren't there in the early stages of long-term projects.

Therefore, the team and individual members of the team need to devise their own motivation. Goals and deadlines are key to keeping the team focused on completing a project as quickly as possible.

Typically, the closer a deadline looms, the more work gets completed. Therefore, develop interim goals and deadlines to get more work done faster. Interim goals will help your team space your work throughout the whole time period, rather than trying to do the usual 80% of the work in the final 20% of total time. This will give you time to adjust your plans, pace your workload, and minimize stress. By getting started earlier on the work, there may be more ways that will shorten the project timeline. Follow the project plan!

Another way to stay motivated and focused is to count down to the next stage gate decision or key interim goal. Don't keep saying you have until a certain date (May 1) to complete a set of tasks. Instead talk in terms of how much time you have left to complete the work (three weeks).

The well-traveled road to success hasn't been fully paved in the development of each new product. It is more of a gravel road with bumps and potholes that occasionally turn into only a two track lane (or less). Sometimes you are out in the forest whacking away at underbrush to find the path. Often you barely maneuver around one obstacle when the next one pops up.

These obstacles tend to create peaks and valleys of progress. Because the research doesn't follow a well-worn path, it is difficult to foresee how many peaks and valleys lie ahead. Research projects have many peaks and valleys, and the valleys can seem to go on forever. It is easy to get discouraged as technical progress is sometimes slow or non-existent.

Don't let this happen to you. Don't just focus on the amplitude of the mountain peaks and valleys, or the Y-axis (Figure 21.1). Use an X-axis perspective and look at the hills and valleys as part of the journey (Figure 21.1). Each valley indicates that the project has moved forward, no matter how discouraging the current results are.

Staying focused on this X-axis perspective will minimize the damaging emotional effects of the valleys of research progress. Remind yourself how far you have come on the project and how many hurdles you have already overcome.

FIGURE 21.1 There Are Peaks and Valleys in a Research Project

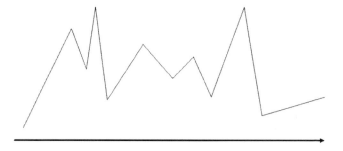

Celebrate the peaks. It's an opportunity to remind everyone that you have reached at least one of the peaks and to enjoy the moment. Each discovery that moves your project forward is important, so always be quick to recognize progress. Do a quick celebration and then get ready to have fun with the next challenge!

Even small celebrations for progress can be a big boost to morale. Researchers like to know that *someone* is making progress on the project, even if they are struggling with their own part. That elevation of the mood may be just what others need to get a new perspective on their part of the project that they are struggling with.

This is especially helpful on those days when forward motion seems to be stalled – and maybe even the project feels like it is stuck in reverse!

A high stress situation is not conducive to creative thinking. By relaxing, you help restore your creativity. Sometimes simply confidence and a "can do" attitude will spark your creativity to move the project forward.

It is easy to slip into a negative frame of mind when there are several experiments in a row where progress isn't obvious. Recognize when this is happening to you, and then figure out how to get re-energized about the project. A positive attitude doesn't guarantee that all problems will be solved, but it tends to increase the odds that you will find a solution much more than a negative attitude.

Here are some ideas you can use to generate your own motivation. Visualize the impact of achieving the end result. Consider how what you are doing will improve the lives of others. Imagine yourself watching the customer smile as the first product is coming off the production line. Imagine your elation and sense of accomplishment when the project is completed. Put up a reminder about WHY you are doing the project and look at it every day.

Use the project as an opportunity to learn and grow in your understanding of the science. Be appreciative of the scientific advances you are making and develop an intuitive feel for the science itself. In the process, you are likely to become a more valuable resource to your company.

QUESTIONS TO ASK:
- How can you keep yourself motivated when the project's forward momentum appears to have stalled, maybe even sliding backward?
- How are you tracking progress?
- What tends to demotivate you?
- How many valleys have you made it through already?
- When was the last time you celebrated success?
- What success can your team celebrate now?
- How is your project going to improve the lives of your customers – and their customers?

22 -- Using Marketplace Demand to Focus Development

Estimating marketplace demand is an important part of faster product development. Companies often create maps (Figure 22.1) to get a better picture of which opportunities to explore first. Usually three key criteria of each potential market application (selling price, volume, and when commercial sales will begin) are presented on one chart using bubbles to represent the volume. This visual is a useful tool in communicating those to work on now and the applications to focus on at a later date.

FIGURE 22.1 Marketplace Demand Map

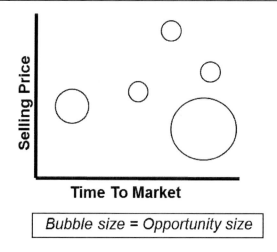

Bubble size = Opportunity size

To create a marketplace demand map, the project team first identifies potential opportunities. This is usually done by a combination of internal and external brainstorming, discussions with potential customers and suppliers, and independent marketing research.

This brainstormed list of potential end use applications is then culled to the top 10-15% potential applications. The project team then further assesses the potential of these top applications.

The key pieces of information that are typically used to assess and prioritize the applications are:

- Marketplace need
- Synergy with existing markets or customers
- Market opening
- Potential volume of unit sales
- Profit/unit
- Competitive advantage
- Ease of market penetration
- Transition from one opportunity to another
- Company market focus
- Liability concerns
- Length of time before sales
- Length of pre-market testing

The most important factor is marketplace need. If there is no need for the product, customers won't be interested in evaluating the product.

Having the team focus a concerted effort on just a limited number of applications will increase the speed to market. Typically, you want to get as much high value business as you can to maximize your profitability. Companies usually develop some larger volume applications to cover the fixed costs of a plant and allow them to build a bigger plant. Usually, the larger a plant, the lower the average unit cost to manufacture a product.

Your team will focus on marketplace openings that are real - legislation that has been passed, for example, not legislation that might be changed. While companies might be interested in talking with you while legislative changes are being discussed, it is only after a change is announced (and before companies need to comply) that you will see the strongest development activity.

Those applications with a marketplace opening allow new products to have a more level playing field against incumbent materials and suppliers. Therefore, your product development team will work to get your product evaluated during these windows of opportunity when companies are doing evaluations of new or modified products.

Your team may have to look at outside contract manufacturers to make your product if you can't manufacture sufficient quantities in-house to quickly meet the needs of the marketplace.

It is common to initially pursue a small application for proof of concept of your product, where failure won't destroy your company's reputation in the marketplace. But if the product doesn't work in the application, companies can sometimes expend too much resources trying to make that small application work, rather than learning what they can and moving on to another application.

Even if you get your product evaluated and approved, you won't be able to keep the business long term without a competitive advantage. A competitive advantage is a point of differentiation for your company or product that the customer recognizes and values. It has to be something that is not easily replicated by your competitors. Your team will get business faster if you focus on applications where your product and company are advantaged.

The competitive advantage can be at the product level (i.e., yours is the only one that can be used at greater than 110°C), the personnel level (i.e., strong relationship with this marketplace segment over the years), or the business or company level (i.e., industry leader in operating room medical devices). Additionally, it could be a cultural aspect of the company (i.e., always easy to work with), or a cost basis (i.e., lowest manufacturing cost), or global supply capability (first to market).

QUESTIONS TO ASK:
- What are the key potential applications for your product?
- What are the current estimated price and volume of your product for each application?
- What is the market opening for each application?
- What is the potential competitive advantage of your product for each application?
- Are any of these applications likely to cluster around one specific product? What would be the aggregate demand for that product?
- What does this information tell your team about how to approach verifying marketplace need for your product/technology?

23 -- Internal Cash Flow and the Importance of Speed to Market

Industries go through economic boom and bust cycles in a fairly predictable pattern. An economic cycle refers to economy-wide fluctuations in production or economic activity over several months or years with the sequence of economic activity typically characterized by expansion, peak, recession, and trough.

These cycles will impact your company's project development budget. There is typically more money available to do research when an industry is booming. The boom years for project development funding are about a third of the industry peak-to-peak cycle time. When an industry starts to go through the bust part of the cycle, the flow of dollars to product development will shrink, often dramatically.

More development projects will be started when times are good for a company than when they aren't. It is easy to start several projects at the same time because in the earliest stages, the cost per project is very low. Most of the earliest work involves talking with others or searching for and analyzing previous research. Neither of these tends to require large outlays of cash or large amounts of expensive equipment.

As you run experiments in the lab and then on larger pieces of equipment, the dollar "burn rate" goes up significantly. (The "burn rate" is the speed at which a company is spending money - or burning through it). As development projects advance, all the departments that are involved in the product development will be increasing their burn rate.

Since many projects will be started at the same time and move forward almost in lockstep in the early phases, a company quickly gets to the point where it can't afford to continue funding all these projects even in good economic times - even factoring in those projects that don't pan out.

But just about the time that many of these development projects hit the scale-up phase of development and need significantly more resources, the company will probably start to feel the effects of an economic slowdown. Therefore, fewer dollars will be available just when the projects need the most funding.

Management will use the stage gate decision process to control the number of projects in each stage. There are typically two parts to each decision. First is whether the project economics warrant moving the project to the next stage. If the answer is yes, then management will determine whether there are enough funds and resources available to do the required work for the next stage of the project.

Those projects for which there isn't adequate funding will be "shelved" (stopped working on) using a Portfolio Management mindset. Typically, the project winners will be those that are furthest along toward commercialization, require fewer dollars to complete, have fewer downside risks, have a high reward, have a greater certainty of success, and have a shorter time before the flow of dollars into company coffers. It is rare that one project is a clear winner in all categories.

Customer interest in purchasing your product gets serious management attention. Therefore, your team wants to get the project far enough down the development path to have a commitment from customers to jointly work on commercial development. While this is no guarantee of maintaining funding, it will likely put you ahead of all projects that lack that commitment.

The faster your team completes each phase, the more likely that management will have the resources available to move your project forward – especially if few other projects have reached that stage.

Moving your project forward faster than the other projects while focusing on reducing technical and marketplace uncertainty will significantly increase the odds that your project's funding will continue. It is also important to figure out ways of minimizing the cost of *further* research, thus increasing the odds that management will move the project forward.

Once you get the green light to move into customer trials and production scale-up, your team should assume that the amount of time and money allocated to your project is the maximum amount you will get and manage accordingly. Make sure your scale-up plans take into account the production schedule of your plant. If your production plant is running at tight capacity, it will be difficult to get time on your company's production equipment for an experimental trial.

QUESTIONS TO ASK:
- How long do you have before product development funding is likely to be reduced within your company?
- What project performance do you have to demonstrate by then?
- Which experiments are critical to the success of the project and thus need to be done first (show stoppers)?
- What are the key milestones?

24 -- How to Stay Focused to Go Faster

Project milestones are a powerful way to keep you focused and moving fast. Following an up-to-date project plan is critical to the success of all projects.

When you hold yourselves accountable to the milestone dates, you will be forced to think through what is really essential for the project and get focused on that. This will then free up your creativity on those essential activities.

Sometimes it does make sense to adjust the milestone. After all, the milestones are just a knowledgeable estimate of how long it *might* take to make the needed discoveries.

For example, the performance parameters from the customers might initially be incomplete as customers work through their requirements (as shown in Figure 17.1). As the project moves forward and additional input (such as competitor product launches, new customer information, and customer evaluations of the new product's performance) is obtained, the final end product performance requirements will often be adjusted. This new information may result in an adjustment to the development timeline.

Whenever a change in performance is identified, quickly incorporate the new requirements into your development plan. The sooner you know the key required performance properties, the faster you can focus your research on a meaningful path. That maximizes your time to research and identify ways to achieve the targeted results.

Most companies that use a stage gate development process will focus on quickly developing prototype products. These prototypes allow customer evaluation and feedback, which provide further information for product refinement.

As the project goes into the development phase, your product team will be pursuing multiple market segments. It is likely that the same product will not meet the performance requirements of all those market segments. As many as three to seven products may ultimately be needed, not just the one that was the initial development target.

Your Project Leadership Team will determine which products to focus on commercializing first, based on customer and business input along with your technical input. The fewer products that you are focusing on developing, the faster you can go.

As your project moves through the development process and gets traction from customers, others in your organization will start to request samples of your material or ask you to make special formations of your product for them. Make sure that all these requests are vetted by your Project Team Leadership before you comply with these requests.

If you spend time developing experimental products for others and don't stay focused on your own project team's commitments, you may find the funds for your project depleted without meeting your milestones. Failing to deliver against milestones will usually result in reduced or eliminated project funding.

This can be a really hard one to handle. It's nice to have others think of your project as successful enough that they want to participate. On the other hand, your team has to be focused on getting the first product commercialized.

If there is a situation where your product has applicability to another important project, then resources may need to be allocated to the other project in addition to yours. If that is the case, your Project Champion and Project Leader will make sure that the appropriate discussions are held with management, tradeoffs are assessed, and decisions are made for resource redeployment and milestone adjustment.

QUESTIONS TO ASK:
- What does your project have to achieve to move it through the next stage gate?
- How long do you have to achieve those results?
- How can you quickly develop a prototype product for customers to evaluate?
- Can you afford to divert your efforts on this project to look at another opportunity for your product and still meet your milestones?
- If not, have you communicated your concerns to your supervisor/project leader?
- What have you learned that will help you shorten the time to complete development?

Part 5

How to Determine Product Viability

25 -- How Customer Value Is Extracted

Your product must deliver value to the customer before the customer will purchase it. The typical ways that a product delivers value are: (1) it allows your customers to provide their customers with improved performance that they can charge more for, (2) it reduces your customers' total costs, or (3) it allows your customer to capture increased market share.

The commercial members of your team (usually your technical customer interface person) will determine what your product enables your customers to do differently and how much value that brings to the customer. For example, if one advantage of your product is its lower density, then that might enable the customer to purchase less material to perform the same function.

The revenue potential that your company can then expect from selling your product will come from two major sources:
- The number of units your company sells
- The price you sell each unit of product for

Breaking out demand into volume and price gives your team a better sense of where the more profitable segments are.

Multiple components affect the selling price of your product, including:
- Selling price of the available competitive alternatives
- Your product's performance versus competitive alternatives
- Supply/demand ratio for your competitor's products (as available supply stays constant and demand increases, prices tend to rise)
- Volume of product being purchased
- Cost of major raw materials used in your product (contracts are often written to allow supplier to pass on raw material price volatility to customers)

Over time, the first to market with a workable solution will typically have 50+% market segment share. The second to market will typically have 20-30% market segment share. Third to market will have about 10%. The rest of the competitors will have just a few percent, combined. These numbers aren't hard and fast for every situation, but they aren't far off, either. For small niches, first to market might have even higher percentages because the size of the application doesn't make it worthwhile for other suppliers to compete.

If you and your competitors are bringing products to the customer at virtually the same time, there is less of a sense of who is first to market. In that case, there might be closer to an even split of the customer's business between your company and the other supplier.

The greater the time lag between qualification of your product and your competitors' later solutions, the stronger your position as first to market. Therefore, it's important to meet your customer's evaluation window in the earliest material qualification cycle, rather than next cycle, whenever you can. Then your product could become the standard against which other products will be measured. Your company's track record for *supplying* a quality product will be compared against later entrants' *promises* to deliver.

Because most customers want a second source of supply to minimize the risk of not having a raw material available in the event that a supplier's plant goes down, you can expect that a second competitor will likely get a small share of the business over time. Experience suggests that the suppliers' split of the business will likely be 80% for the first supplier and 20% for the backup supplier. Customers usually appreciate the time and effort that a supplier initially takes to help a customer solve a problem. The reward/repayment is usually the share of the customer's business and sometimes a *slightly* higher price than an alternate supplier.

Your company does not capture all the value that your products bring to the customer because:

- Your customers have expenses and ongoing risks associated with the use of your product that they want to be compensated for.
- Other competitive products in the marketplace have driven the price/performance expectations to a lower point.
- How customers calculate their costs doesn't allow them to recognize some of the added benefit of your product.

Whenever customers use a new material, they risk unknown negative consequences of using the product. They also have to spend time testing and re-qualifying with their customers using your new product. Customers expect to keep a share of the value as compensation for both.

Before you introduce your new product into the marketplace, your customer already has a spectrum of products available with various performance attributes. This is how potential customers see that price/ performance grid.

FIGURE 25.1 Price – Performance Grid

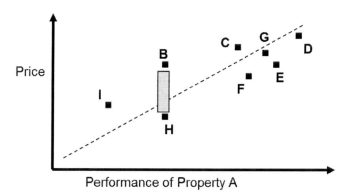

Although it isn't a perfectly straight line, in general, price tends to increase as performance increases.

If the estimated performance of Property A for your new product is around where Products B and H are on the chart, you might assume that your target pricing will be at Product B pricing. But unless your new product also has the characteristic performance of Product B, a more conservative assumption is that the selling price of your product will be that of Product H or even lower than the selling price of H.

How can this be possible? By bringing your product into the marketplace, you are increasing competition, which will drive prices lower. Let's look at Product B, for example. Perhaps they have been enjoying a price premium because they were the only company that could make a polymer with a desired combination of properties.

Now if your new product will compete with Product B, which already has a track record with the customer, your product will be riskier for the customer at the time they decide to switch because of all the unknowns about your product's performance that were mentioned earlier.

It isn't uncommon to have the incumbent supplier of Product B watch to see if a competitive product gets qualified at the customer. When it looks like the second product will be equally effective, the competitor making incumbent Product B can choose to cut its price just enough to stop customers from purchasing from the second supplier. This will effectively lower the selling price of Product B.

As you can see from this discussion, extracting value for your product can be difficult. You will help your company's sales representative in these negotiations by articulating the benefits of your product versus each competitor's product.

QUESTIONS TO ASK:
- What does the price/performance grid for competitors to your product look like?
- What value does your product have versus the customer's incumbent product?
- What are your team's current plans for determining the viability of your new product based on your understanding of the price/performance grid?
- What factors are your customers considering when deciding the value of switching to your product?
- How is this impacting the value that the customer recognizes and, therefore, the pricing your team can expect?

26 -- How to Reduce Costs

Once you have developed a product that meets your customer's needs, the focus will shift to driving down the cost to produce the product.

Using a very simple model, Figure 26.1 illustrates why the maximum cost to manufacture your product needs to be much lower than the selling price for your product to be profitable.

You start with the selling price that you can get for your product. You then subtract selling, research, and administrative (SRA) overhead expenses which we are assuming to be 10% (typically this ranges from 2 – 25% for established products). We subtract 30% for taxes, interest payments, and depreciation of equipment. We also subtract a 10% profit target (typically this is 5 - 20% for companies). The result is that our target manufacturing cost must be less than 50% of the selling price of our competitive product. If the product will sell for $1.00 per pound, our manufacturing cost would have to be less than $0.50 per pound. As you can see from this example there is a big difference between the manufacturing cost and a profitable selling price.

FIGURE 26.1 Estimating Maximum Manufacturing Cost

Cost Structure	Percent of Selling Price
Selling Price	100
Less: SRA	10
Less: Taxes, Interest, Depreciation	30
Less: Profit target	10
Maximum manufacturing cost	50

Initial sample quantities that are sent to customers will typically sell for far less that the cost to make them in a "pilot" (small, pre-production scale) plant. Therefore, supplying from a small scale manufacturing facility isn't an effective long-term strategy. The primary purpose of these initial sample quantities is to seed the market for future profitable sales from a production scale facility, not to make a profit on the early samples themselves.

Through an iterative process involving input from research, marketing, and manufacturing, your economic analyst will provide an initial estimate of the size of the manufacturing plant needed to give your project the required manufacturing economics (Figure 26.2). This early manufacturing estimate will help in selecting applications to pursue and in determining areas of the production process that need further research to lower the manufacturing costs. Your analyst will further refine the model as more market and technical data become available.

FIGURE 26.2 Maximum Cost for Commercial Viability

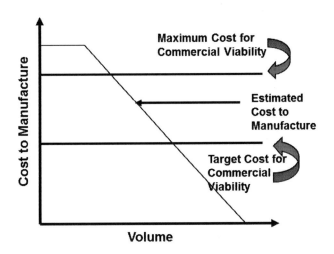

The dollars invested in development impact profitability. The money that is spent by your team to develop your product isn't free money.

Your company has to pay to borrow that money, either through interest charges to banks or a dividend to stockholders until the products your team develops generate revenue. If the average borrowing cost (debt and equity financing) is 12% and it takes you an additional five years to develop the product for commercial sales, then for your company to break even on those costs during the first year of commercial sale, you will need $176,234 in profit in the first year of commercial sales for every $100,000 spent in the first year of the project development ($100,000 x $1.12^5 = $176,234$) to recover each initial $100,000 outlay plus the interest charges paid.

These costs are paid back through use of the profits your company makes from selling your products. Of course, companies don't expect to pay back all the R&D expenses in the first year of commercialization. This example is just for illustrative purposes about the time value of investments when companies borrow funds to complete research.

The more dollars that are spent to develop a product and the longer it takes to generate profits, the more expensive a project is to a company because there is more accumulated interest.

Therefore, two key ways that you as a researcher impact project costs are how quickly you develop a product that meets customers' needs and how fast you can develop a production process that reduces the cost to safely and reliably make the product in a production plant.

There will generally be lower development costs if the product is developed faster, because people will be working more efficiently and less management time will be needed to run the project. This requires great communication between team members, including knowing who needs the output handed off to them and by when to do their job better. Many teams put together input/output information flows to know who is doing the work, who needs to be consulted before the work is done, and who needs to get the output after the work is completed. This significantly reduces missed handoffs of information that can slow a project down.

QUESTIONS TO ASK:
- What is your estimated target manufacturing cost?
- What is the minimum size production plant needed to profitably make your product?
- How can you quickly reduce the cost of safely and reliably making this new product in production?
- How can you improve the transfer of information to and from research to speed up the project development?

27 -- Skill Sets Needed by Researchers

This chapter covers several valuable, non-science skills for researchers to develop: a sense of urgency, focus with flexibility, communication skills, and being a good team player.

Development projects have longer time horizons than other company activities. Over time there can be a tendency to be satisfied with minimal progress. To avoid this tendency, you need to use your own internal clock to develop a sense of urgency. Some key questions to keep you working faster are:

- Can you learn to do this faster?
- Should you be working on this yet?
- Whose help will you need soon and will they be available?
- How much of this work can you parallel process?
- How do you minimize your time on your project's critical path?
- How can you communicate better to make sure nothing is being missed?
- What is the customer's targeted performance?
- What are the criteria for management in your company to say yes to the project stage gate?
- Which of your tasks are most critical?
- Which tasks are you working on now?

Use your milestones and critical issues in the multifunctional project plan to keep focused on the most important activities. Focus on doing the few vital things. Constantly search and watch for changes that could impact the project – either negatively or positively.

Look for any information you can leverage along the way. Look for ideas and suggestions that will allow you to do your work better, faster, and easier. Plan ahead for the next steps, anticipate any upcoming changes, and plan contingencies for those changes.

Being able to communicate effectively is critical. You will interact with people inside and outside your company to complete your project. Learn to use all the electronic tools at your disposal to get information disseminated as quickly as possible.

During a presentation, clearly communicate the key pieces of information in the way that the decision makers prefer. This will maximize the probability that a decision will be made quickly. Have additional information readily available in case you are asked for it.

Be a good team player. Always be willing to give another team member a hand – wherever you can - to keep them on track. Be prepared to go to bat for team members, when needed, to make sure that they have the time and resources to do their job well.

Ask for help for what you don't know how to do. Otherwise, you will be slowing down your project while you try to learn something that others could have quickly and easily told you.

What is your weakest skill? Do you know someone who is great at it (or at least better at it than you)? Can he or she teach you how to do it?

Being an effective team member requires knowing and abiding by ground rules for meetings (staying on task, time keeping, virtual meeting log-in times) and team norms (common access site for team information, how to word e-mails when fast response is needed, turnaround time on requests.)

Learning and applying these skills will help you be an effective team player.

28 -- Line Extension Products

The research on a minor modification of an existing product, such as changing the amount of an additive by 0.1% in a formulation, will be well understood because of all the previous research that people in your company have done in this area. Because these typically use materials already approved for this application, there is significantly less research activity needed to run the product in production and to get customer approval.

Far more research work is needed with more complicated line extensions. Line extension products usually are based on a chemistry that your company already uses in commercial products. You then will build on that fundamental technology to create your modified product.

Many times these types of products are initiated when your company's existing product no longer meets customers' needs.

Much of the infrastructure (such as production plant and R&D equipment) to complete line extensions projects will already be in place. A minimum of production plant changes will be needed since you will be primarily working with the same base product. Since customer relationships are already established, the commercial organization in your company will understand the needs of your target customers well and have good working relationships with them.

All of these enable your development team to quickly develop a product that meets the required performance. Because so much can be leveraged, these research projects usually require only a few months to a couple years to complete.

You will still have to verify with your legal department that you are "free to practice" the modified product. You will also want to determine if you have developed a patentable product or if what you developed should remain a trade secret.

All the steps we have discussed will apply to your modified product. You may find that you can move through some of the steps quickly because of prior research, but it is important that you address each question separately for your product and verify that all steps are completed.

29 -- New-to-the-World Products

Your company will usually develop a new-to-the-world (NTTW) technology for one of two reasons: either chemical exploration has uncovered a new route to making a chemical, or an unmet marketplace demand requires a new product to meet the need.

NTTW technology usually takes many years to develop into a commercial product because so many unknowns have to be addressed before the product can be commercialized.

When looking backward on a longer term research progress, this is how technical progress looks based on end product performance (Figure 29.1).

FIGURE 29.1 New-to-the-World Product Performance

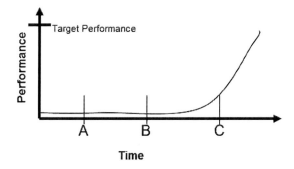

In these situations, teams will focus on intermediate goals and milestones for developing the fundamental technology using the project plan. This allows management to have something other than just final product performance to effectively assess the project's progress.

You will also find that because the product is NTTW, customers for the product will be slow in adopting it (adoption curve). They will try it in only one line of their products, watch how it performs, and then slowly start using your product in other lines. The adoption curve is slower for new products than it is for minor modifications of existing products.

Sometimes NTTW chemicals are used in NTTW end-use applications, which are also going through a slow adoption curve of their own. The tradeoff for patience in the adoption for new end uses is that once your product is specified into the application, you will not likely be displaced. Since your customer will have only your material to use, your customer's product will be developed around your product's capabilities.

If your product is the only one that is effective in a specific application, your company will have an opportunity to extract greater value for your product and recoup your development costs quicker.

Now it's time for you to apply what you have learned in this book and create some marvelous products that will help make the world a better place and make your company more profitable because you were there. I wish you fast and successful development of all your products!

How to Engage With Me

You were hired by your company for your experience and capabilities in certain scientific areas. Yet success in product development goes beyond the science. When you are new to commercial research, it can seem daunting to understand how all these areas of product development fit together.

But with someone to help guide you, it becomes much easier and more fun.

My commitment is that this straightforward approach to product development will provide you with measurable results. You can spend your time more efficiently and optimize your research. The approach outlined in this book is designed to be fully aligned with your company's existing work process.

If there are areas of faster product development that you want further information about, even if I didn't address it in this book, please let me know. I would love to hear from you. Your success is important to me.

Either send an e-mail to Teresa@ResearchDoneRight.com or call me at 989-600-1052 (8:00 a.m. - 5:00 p.m. EST).

About The Author

Teresa M. O'Brien helps chemists and engineers who want to get their products to market quicker by focusing on the key elements for success beyond the science. Teresa is the founder and President of *O'Brien Consulting Group, LLC* and enjoys working with individuals and organizations to get their products to market sooner.

Teresa has worked in the trenches doing laboratory product development, pilot plant and production plant scale-up work, marketing research for potential new products, leading new product development teams, and coaching new product development teams for a Fortune 50 company and one of the largest chemical and plastics manufacturers in the world.

As creator of "Research Done Right," she teaches scientists who want to launch successful products, helping them understand the elements beyond the science that are as necessary as the science itself for a successful product launch. She offers one-on-one coaching and e-learning to help chemists and engineers gain the knowledge, support, and resources they need, providing a roadmap that ***gets results***.